Grant Writing

for Christian Ministries
&
Nonprofit Organizations

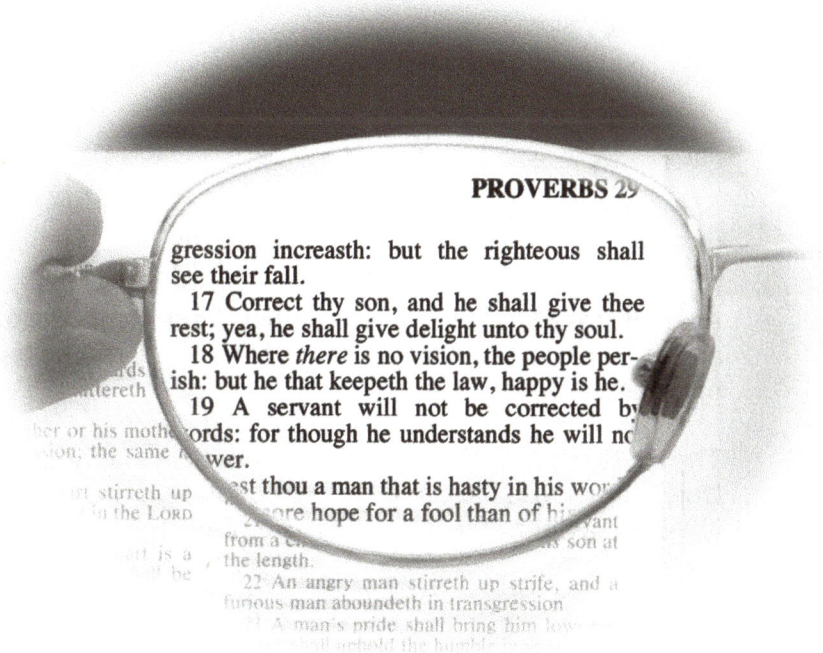

PROVERBS 29

gression increaseth: but the righteous shall see their fall.

17 Correct thy son, and he shall give thee rest; yea, he shall give delight unto thy soul.

18 Where *there* is no vision, the people perish: but he that keepeth the law, happy is he.

19 A servant will not be corrected by words: for though he understands he will no...

...st thou a man that is hasty in his wo...

...ore hope for a fool than of hi...

...the length.

22 An angry man stirreth up strife, and a furious man aboundeth in transgression

MICHAEL L. STICKLER

Grant Writing for Christian Ministries
Author Michael L. Stickler

Copyright ©2018 Michael L. Stickler

ISBN 978-0-9907441-8-4

Published by:

The VisionGROUP LTD
www.TheVisionGroupLtd.com
MikeStickler.online

Grant Writing
for Christian Ministries and Nonprofits
TABLE OF CONTENTS

I will show you what he is like who comes to me and hears my words and puts them into practice. He is like a man building a house, who dug down deep and laid the foundation on rock. When a flood came, the torrent struck that house but could not shake it, because it was well built. But the one who hears my words and does not put them into practice is like a man who built a house on the ground without a foundation. The moment the torrent struck that house, it collapsed and its destruction was complete. (Luke 6: 47-49, NIV)

Introduction

When it comes to:
- defining and facilitating your organization's grant or contract funding,
- creating a giving and generous culture within your church,
- developing a culture of evangelism in your congregation or ministry,
- engaging in dialog with vision-led foundations and donors,
- attracting funding to a partnership in your organization's vision,
- beginning a large capital accumulation campaign, or
- developing and communicating your vision as the heart of fundraising, volunteer development, and community engagement, our training, research, and our experience, have led us to this basic observation: there are three sets of foundational statements that underlie the actions of any organization.

Whether the organization is trying to serve, expand, find reliable resource support, or build new capacity -- from the smallest and most casual to the largest and most highly sophisticated -- every organization rests upon these three sets of foundational statements. And every organization is guided by them -- to success or to failure. Your church is no different.

In those cases where these statements are unwritten, unshared, and inconsistent (although they still, in fact, exist and are implicit in the actions of the organization), their inconsistency and fuzziness usually lead the organization to chaos and failure.

Generally (and in contrast), successful organizations craft these statements in clear and explicit terms – and cast them in written and widely distributed forms (at least internally) so their corporate action is clearly guided and highly focused.

These three sets of foundational statements are the organization's ...

purpose statements, its

planning statements, and its

process statements.

Consider the importance of these foundational statements to an organization that has existed for more than 2,000 years. An organization of people – some publicly associated with it and some not so clearly identified. Consider the larger Christian Church – both the Church Visible and the Church Invisible. Recorded in the Gospels of Matthew and of Luke, Jesus said -- to His chosen twelve, to the large crowd of His disciples who were there, and a great number of people from all over Judea, from Jerusalem, and from the coast of Tyre and Sidon, who had come to hear Him:

> Therefore, everyone who hears these words of mine and puts them into practice is like a wise man who built his house on the rock. The rain came down, the streams rose, and the winds blew and beat against that house; yet it did not fall, because it had its foundation on the rock. But everyone who hears these words of mine and does not put them into practice is like a foolish man who built his house on sand. The rain came down, the streams rose, and the winds blew and beat against that house, and it fell with a great crash. (Matthew 7: 24-27, NIV)

The fundamental choice, then, is clear:

– build your church upon the rock of clear and explicit foundational statements and ensure that all of its members are guided by them ...

-- or –

– build your church upon the sand of inconsistent and fuzzy statements and leave its members guessing.

At the Vision Group, we choose the rock – explicit statements of purpose, of plans, and of processes to focus and guide our organization – our clients' organizations – and the alliances of organizations it takes to achieve transformational change in neighborhoods, cities, regions – and the world.

In the next few pages, we identify the three layers to this foundational rock -- these three sets of foundational statements. And we define our terms and teach on the most important. We leave teaching on the rest for an extensive development in other sessions. We help organizations apply these concepts to their specific situations through consulting services.

Are you ready to "rock" your world?

Concepts, and language, and terms – oh my!

First, the quick overview – the foundational concepts, language, and terms in a thumbnail sketch definition form:

Purpose. The most fundamental of these three sets of foundational statements, in fact, are the statements of the very reason for the existence of the organization itself. Their crafting and casting are the exclusive responsibility of the organization's owner.

The most fundamental of these three sets of foundational statements are the purpose statements: Values, Mission, Market, and Vision. They underlie the other fundamental statements and all of the organization's actions. In fact, the best short description of any organization is an integrated expression of these most fundamental statements –

> "We are (our values) who accomplish (our mission) for (our market) so that (our vision of a better future for our community) is achieved."

Planning. Resting on the purpose statements are the statements that address the question of "How?" These statements bring the purpose of the organization into a context of deliberate reality for the organization:

- defining the necessary tasks, resources and relationships necessary to do them;

- addressing how these relationships will be developed; and

- addressing how these resources will be attracted, timed, and organized

… to accomplish the mission in the targeted market -- thus achieving the vision in the service area. Their crafting and casting are the responsibility of the organization's leadership.

The *planning* set of foundational statements – the **Strategies, Plans, and Goals** for resources (human, information, and physical), marketing, partnering, operations, and future development -- identify and define the work of the organization. They specifically address all of the things necessary to exist as an organization, relate to the community it serves and in which it resides, and attract its resources, allies, and its clients.

Processes. Finally, resting on both the purpose and planning statements, are the statements of the intended actions of the organization – actions taken over time which combine and regulate the use of resources to the needs of the customers -- effectively and efficiently. Their crafting, deployment, operation, effectiveness and efficiency testing, and re-design (over the long and short terms) is the responsibility of the organization's leadership – and its expertise (especially those who will practice them) and the customers.

The **process** set of foundational statements capture the design and implementation of the plans at the operating level and for each process, defines the action sequences and resource use to effect deliberate changes in the lives of the process's customer. And, as these customer outcomes are observed over time – and as the environment, the customer, and the field's best practices change -- they re-design and improve the processes to bring the customers' life changes into greater and more persistent conformance with the intended outcomes. People, working through processes accomplish the mission. The increasing numbers of changed lives they produce achieve the vision.

Although his examples may offend, Malcolm Gladwell's observations of the secular world, which led him to this basic thesis in his book *The Tipping Point*, is intuitively helpful in understanding the leverage: little changes can have big effects; when small numbers of people start behaving differently, that behavior can ripple outward until a critical mass or "tipping point" is reached, after which changing the world is inevitable.

What do we really mean by all of these terms?

Playwright George Bernard Shaw claimed that "England and America are two countries divided by a common language." If only today's management literature were that simple.

But rather than speak in the management literature's baffle-gab and be dazzled by its buzzwords, let's be sure that we all understand the concepts that underlie the terms we use. Many of these terms have a long history (and widely differentiated meanings) in the modern management literature – which can quickly become a barrier to our common understanding. If we are to reason together (Isaiah 1:18), we need to ensure that we use a common language in our sessions and in our practices. As the Bible claims that *"All Scripture is God-breathed and is useful for teaching, rebuking, correcting and training in righteousness, so that the man of God may be thoroughly equipped for every good work"* (2 Tim 3:16 -17), we will clarify some terms with its instruction.

Here are the words and the concepts we use:

Purpose terms —

Your Organization -- The people: who are identifiably associated in some manner, who are equipped with physical and informational resources to perform coordinated actions to meet the purpose of your organization, and who (whether paid or unpaid) receive some form of reward for their contribution.

Your allies-Other organizations or people who join with your organization to help it meet its purpose -- or to meet an even greater purpose.

Community -- All of the people who reside in the area in which your organization, its members, its allies, and/or its market reside. Other words may be substituted -- that indicate the size of the community: neighborhood, city, region, country, "global," etc.

Market – Two meanings –
- that segment of the total population of your community from which your organization draws those whom it serves (i.e., its customers, clients, patients, members, etc.) – or –
- that segment of the total population of your community from which your organization draws those whom support it (i.e., its allies, supporters, participants, and donors).

Mission -- what your organization "does" – what it accomplishes for, or provides to its customers, clients, patients, members, etc.

Outcomes -- the changes in the life of your customers, clients, patients, members, etc. as a result of your organization accomplishing its mission

Vision -- the biggest change in the life of the community that can possibly be achieved -- if your mission is completely accomplished.

Values -- what your organization respects and practices / how your organization operates.

Planning terms —

Strategy -- a general operating guidance or method -- usually selected from a broad range of option choices

Plan -- the method of accomplishing part of the mission or a task. A plan implements a strategy. A plan identifies, organizes, and regulates the use of resources on a schedule and by way of a specific set of operating methods to accomplish its assignment by a specific time (a time-oriented plan) or by the when a specific event occurs (an event-oriented plan).

Goals -- a specific and defined set of accomplishments, usually defined for a future completion by or before the occurrence of a specific event or time (event-oriented goals or time-oriented goals, respectively), having used specifically allocated/dedicated amounts of resources. Goals remind us of the importance and urgency of taking focused action – now!

Process terms —

Process -- a specific set of actions taken and decisions made in a designed sequence by which an input of specified resources is changed into an output of specified products made or specified services delivered.

> *Note: Because of:*
>   - variation over time or among process inputs;
>   - learning over time about the reliability of the process design, its operation, and what it produces;
>   - change over time in the environment in which the process operates; and/or
>   - change over time or among customers in their need for the output,
> *… the process must be continually refined to remain useful.*

Such refinement is aimed at:
- maximizing the reliability of the output to fully meeting its customer's need (effectiveness) -- and
- minimizing the generation of waste in the process, minimizing the failure to meet the customer's need, and minimizing the input resource demand (efficiency).

Stewardship -- a deliberate and continuing action -- of re-designing the process to increase its effectiveness and its efficiency by measuring the outputs against the customer's short- and long-term need and the input resource use -- and using these data to change the process to drive the changes in it to accomplish these goals.

Bonus term —

One of today's emerging buzzwords is "transformation" – and its many siblings: transform, transformed, transformational. Seized by the popular management literature as a latest new thing, it carries a myriad of meanings -- to the point that now, rather than clarify, this great word simply confuses. In less than nine hundredths of a second, Google finds about 524,000 hits for "Transformational Leadership" alone – with meanings all over the map. We prefer the biblical meaning, rooted in the Greek μεταμορφόω (metamorphoo) -- also translated as "transfigured." Ralph Earle, Th.D. (Word Meanings in the New Testament), writes that the three uses of μεταμορφόω in the New Testament give crucial insight into its meaning:

> On the Mount of Transfiguration (in the parallel passages of Matthew 17:2 and Mark 9:2,), the glory of Jesus burst through the veil of flesh and the disciples caught a glimpse of His eternal glory. Just so, when we are filled with the Holy Spirit, something of the divine glory within will shine out through our lives.

> (Romans 12:2) indicates that transfiguration (transformation) comes through the renewing of one's mind. The (Greek) verb is in the present imperative. It therefore means: 'Go on being continually transfigured (more and more, day by day).' This comes by the constant renewing of our minds. Philippians 4:8 gives some idea of this process.

> The third passage (2 Corinthians 3:17-18) suggests that transfiguration (transformation) takes place as we reflect the glory of God, just as the moon reflects the light of the sun …

As we understand these passages, then, personal transformation is a profound change – to something we could never be done by ourselves or though our own actions or work – and – is something that begins when we accept Christ and continues until we leave this earth. This component– the need for an external/divine input – is critical to our understanding "transformation" in an organizational or community sense. So, for our purposes:

> Transformation -- a profound change for the good, is both
> a state <u>and</u> a process – and – it cannot happen without
> an external/divine input action.

VISION:
The Heart of the Topic

"Where there is no vision, the people perish"

Proverbs 29:18 KJV

Human interaction occurs through relationships. The most powerful of these relationships are vision-based relationships ...

Vision is the key to action. It inspires, motivates, guides... Do not underestimate the power of vision.

> "I only regret that I have but one life to give for my country."
> Nathan Hale, September 1776

If the need is imminent... and the vision is clear...*even volunteers will die for its achievement.*

An Exercise:

With these concepts, language, and terms definitions in hand, and without referring to your organizations literature or your previous notes, please spend a few moments reflecting on your church. Be as specific as you can. Jot down your reflections, date them, and keep them handy – even if you have done this exercise before:

- Who are the people that your organization serves?

- What part of their needs does your organization address?

- How does your organization address those needs?

- What is the area in which your organization, its supporters, and the people whom it serves reside?

- What change in the lives of the people your organization serves does your church hope to make as a result of what it does for them?

- How long does your organization expect these changes to persist in their lives?

- If your organization would be able to make the lasting changes it seeks in the lives of as many of the people whom you could possible serve in the area in which you reside, how would your community's life be changed?

You recognize the *purpose* statements in your responses to these questions. From them, write a short, vision-based description of your organization in this form:

> "We are (our **values**) who accomplish (our **mission**) for (our **market**) so that (our **vision** of a better future in our community) is achieved by (our **goal**)."

Vision Deployment

A warning:

"Vision lasts only 29 days."

--Christian pollster, George Barna,

Raise Your Vision, 2009

George Barna's warning clearly tells us that like faith, vision, without deployment, is dead. Recognizing that all action is based in relationships – and that the most powerful of these are vision-based, Vision Deployment is the cornerstone of every ministry, every organization, even every congregation. Our Vision Development Matrix, which we present in all of our forums, is our guideline. It demonstrates how to share your vision with others.

VISION DEPLOYMENT

Own It	**Partner**
If it's going to be…	*… it has to be through me.*
Catch It	**Constituent**
Asking questions	*Giving sacrificially*
See It	**Donor**
Touch it, Feel it, Smell it	*May give pocket Change*
Hear It	**Prospects**
Introduce them for the first time	*Have never heard of your vision*

It is based on the principle that calling others to action is not about manipulation -- it is about building relationships based on the vision of your church. The steps in the development of this matrix will help you share your vision and then reap the benefits of vision-based action – as co-laborers making the vision happen through your church with the use of their time, talent, and treasure. As we follow along, see this matrix build from the bottom up.

The bottom layer – first actions.

Prospect. At the first stage of your relationship, "they" will be a prospect and will never have heard your vision (or if they have, they may not understand it at all).

Hear It. Your first task is to share the vision! Communicate it simply -- through your newsletter, website, or a conversation. Tell them what you do and why you are passionate about it.

The second layer – relationship forming actions.

See It. The second step is to invite them to see the vision in action. Encourage them to visit the facility, or invite them to a gathering where they can meet the people you help. You want them to touch the vision, feel the vision, and smell the vision -- for themselves -- as it is being played out.

Donor. (This stage recognizes their probable emotional reactions to your organization's good work.) Whether they feel guilt, sadness, or sudden sympathy, they will have heard just enough that their "mercy strings" are pulled. As a response, they usually feel compelled to give whatever they can to assuage these feelings – quickly! These gifts are an excess for them and don't require much effort. These are usually a one-time gifts and we call them what they are for them -- Pocket Change – but don't let them stop here. Bring them further into the relationship, further into engaging the vision.

The third layer – relationship development actions

Catch It. In this stage of understanding, their imagination gets challenged – and employed. Because you have already told them about your vision and they have seen it for themselves, help them explore the vision – intellectually and experientially -- through questions and answers and direct participation within the scope of their gifts.

Constituent. (By definition, "an essential part"). When they reach into themselves to contribute in meaningful amounts of their time, talent, and treasure, they begin to play integral roles in the organization's growth. Their participation will represent personal decisions that have challenged their other plans and their gifts will become sacrificial. As Pastor Eric Brown says at Imago Dei church in Seattle, "Giving isn't giving until it interrupts your lifestyle." A constituent will joyfully give -- of time and money -- to further the vision, no matter what changes they have to implement to make it possible.

The top layer – relationship maturity actions.

Own It. Finally, lead them to where they make your vision their vision. Help them becomes totally involved, that their attitude is one of complete dedication. You won't have to ask them to volunteer or to give, because their natural response is, "How can I?" The "own it" stage is exactly the maturity level of the relationships you maintain with all of your supporters.
Partner. A partner owns the vision 100%. A partner doesn't just say, "How can I," but they have a heart of "How I can." You can be sure that if any crisis or need befell your ministry, your partner will stand by your side through the thick of it.

Partner. A partner owns the vision 100%. A partner doesn't just say, "How can I," but they have a heart of "How I can." You can be sure that if any crisis or need befell your ministry, your partner will stand by your side through the thick of it.

Conclusion

Lacking a vision, all that is left is need. This is not merely semantics. Everyone recognizes and acknowledges need, whether that is spiritual, emotional, physical, or educational. In the face of the crushing needs in the world around us, need is depressing and overwhelming. Vision, on the other hand, is inspiring, motivating, and energizing. Your ability to address a need or to solve a problem rests on the strength, clarity, and effectiveness of your vision.

An Overview of Fundraising in General

Why Fundraising?

We generally understand how a free-market economy works – you buy the goods and services you want or need in a simple, two-party transaction between the producer/seller and the buyer/consumer. When the transaction is complete, you are happy with what you bought and the producer is happy with what they were paid for it.

As you have worked (i.e., exchanging your time and talent for your employer's treasure), you have the means to buy. In our economic system, what you buy is generally priced higher than what it cost to deliver it – and that difference between price and cost is "profit" or wealth – which in our economic system, the owners are allowed to keep as their incentive to work – to even greater effect. These producers of the goods and services we buy at a price more than the cost are the for-profit firms who make up the supply side of our economy. They are expected to maximize the owners' reward for their work.

This system works very well. On the supply side of our economy, the for-profit firms create all of the economic wealth in our economy out of God's abundance – and generally fill all of the consumers' wants and needs.

But this system is not perfect.

For some (and this includes us), the need is simply too great or too diffused to figure out how to buy its solution on an individual basis. For example, consider roads, or common defense, or peaceful dispute resolutions … the things we relegate to the functions of our governments).

And for some members of our community (for whatever reason), they have not or cannot either earn or spend the money it takes to buy what they want, or need – maybe even at their subsistence level.

For us, these are the "poor" (whom Jesus said would always be with us). These are the ones whom we are to feed, clothe, give drink, visit in prison... we have a personal responsibility to them -- to fill their needs out of the abundance God has given to us.

In either case, we have two choices: care for all of these people personally (supplying the goods and services they need on our own) or, organize in some way to have these goods and services supplied on our behalf -- achieving, perhaps, economy of scale and even providing the goods and services (through professionals) better than we can provide them ourselves, individually.

If we choose to organize, the existence of our organization will rely on another transaction model in our free market system – a model designed to replace the two party transaction model where the free market fails with one that accommodates the reality of the consumer's inability to act as their own buyer. This is a three-party transaction model in which the producer provides goods and services to the consumer and a third party (the funder – from the wealth they have created) pays the producer for these deliveries, thus fulfilling their responsibility to "the poor" – or our collective "too big" need.

In our society, these organizations are expected to maximize their delivery of goods and services within the resources available to them – just as the funders are expected to maximize the effectiveness of the wealth with which they support them. The funders (as though their responsibility to "the poor" is not enough) are even incentivized to fund some of these organization (through breaks in the taxes with which they fund the other organizations, i.e., governments). And the non-government provider-organizations are generally relieved from all tax burdens and are not allowed to enrich their owners economically. These latter organizations are thus termed: nonprofit organizations.

Note: All government and nonprofit organizations are funded from the wealth created in the for-profit, supply side of our economy.

So... why the fundraising?

The old pastor's observation to his congregation: "God provides for all our needs – our minor accounting challenge, here, is to convince you to move the wealth you created from His abundance into the places where it will fulfill His purposes for us all."

How do we take up this "minor accounting challenge?"

When groups think of fundraising, they immediately (and sometimes painfully) recall car washes, bake sales, walk-a-thons, or just plain begging. While each of those have their time and place, professional fundraising is far more of a balancing act of different activities, each of which has its own purpose, pros, and cons. In fact, a quality fundraising program could more accurately be called a "community development" program since you need to integrate broad community involvement in every program and at every level of your nonprofit organization.

In fundraising terms, the opposite of vision is need – and in most nonprofits, need has long been the "default" fundraising approach. A great deal of energy goes into convincing church members, local community members and organizations, and foundations of how great the need or problem is so they will give to fix the need.

Need-based appeals are guilt-based appeals.

Need overwhelms. When people feel overwhelmed, they project that on everyone else, including your nonprofit. The more desperate a picture you deliver to motivate giving, the more you overwhelm your audience.

Vision-based appeals uplift--to achievement that is are bigger than life.

Our experience has shown that while need-based appeals work in good economic times, vision-based appeals work better – and all of the time.

Intuitively – how would you respond to a need-based appeal? After all, when times are tough, do you need *more guilt* in your life?

Focus, Focus, Focus
on your Values, Mission, Market, Vision, Goals

People and organizations are most effective when they're focused on a goal. While many people asking for money think they know their goals, when you push them for details they often squirm because they can only offer vague, - often way-too-broad - statements. Clearly defining each can take time, but it can also bring incredible focus and relief to individuals as well as the entire organization. Why? Because folks now know their target, which means they can ignore everything else without feeling guilty.

> "We are (our **values**) who accomplish (our **mission**) for (our **market**) so that (our vision of a better future in our community) is achieved by (our goal)."

First of all, each of these aspects of your philosophy is distinctly different. Understanding the differences can help you better define what you're doing, when, why, and how. They can help you to prioritize your tasks, eliminate distractions, and fast-track valuable opportunities.

But, please… do NOT confuse any of these four with a catchy marketing phrase. Marketing phrases are temporary ways to communicate your philosophy based on the trends of your target market. Values, Market, Mission, Vision, and Goals will define your organization and become part of its identity.

Money Follows Relationships:

Friend-raising and Fund-raising

In the minds of many nonprofit executives and boards, grants are seen as the "magic bullet" to their fundraising woes. Grants are a wonderful source of revenue to grow your organization or program, to initiate something new, or even to start up a new, well-planned agency. But, healthy fundraising is a lot like healthy investing – diversity is the key to success.

This means that you want to regularly receive donations of goods, services, and money from a variety of sources. While this diversity of funding sources includes grants from private foundations and from government agencies – *it also includes donors responding to your:*

newsletter appeals, lunch meetings, dinner socials, big banquets, phone-a-thons, planned giving, major donor developments, and special campaigns.

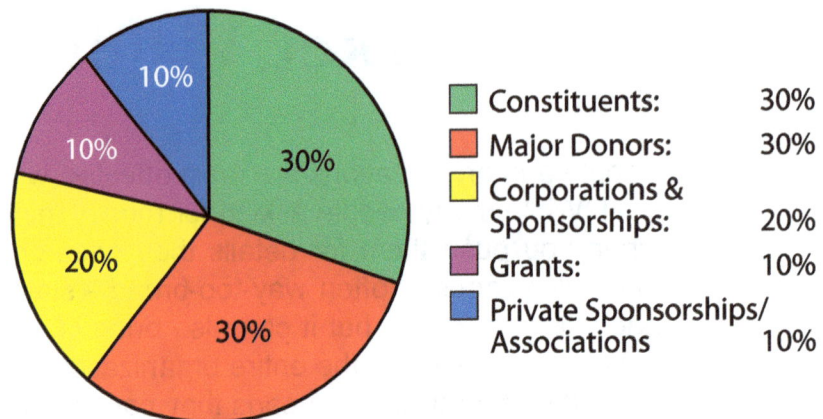

Constituents:	30%
Major Donors:	30%
Corporations & Sponsorships:	20%
Grants:	10%
Private Sponsorships/ Associations	10%

It is the responsibility of nonprofit leaders to diversify their organization's revenue streams. It will look like this:

"But this is about grant writing! I'll never meet those people."

Grant writing as a part of your fundraising plan can be valuable. Grant writing instead of other fundraising efforts is doomed to fail. Funding diversity demonstrates a broad validation of your vision and mission within your community. Grant makers will not support your work if you cannot demonstrate that your community and constituents also do so.

Having healthy support from donors in many areas provides you both a strong foundation for providing services – and a basis for more robust grant proposals.

As we begin to learn what a grant is and how to acquire one, we must keep it in perspective. If your organization expects too much of grant support, the foundations and others to whom you apply will recognize this and your proposal will be denied. Grant makers want to help, but they don't want to carry the whole load! Allowing this understanding will help you develop a respectful relationship with a potential funder.

On the issue of fundraising, the question is, "Which comes first, big dollars or big commitments?" Every healthy, successful organization is founded on relationships. Odds are you had people believing in and working for you before any significant dollars were involved. Countless social organizations grew out of volunteers working out of someone's house (church service at the local senior center), or a borrowed room at the local church or library (adult literacy education), or perhaps from a car, truck, or van (feed/clothe the homeless), or even the local park (after school programs for teens). Rarely does any program start with lots of money and little else; quite the opposite is true.

Interestingly, a 2002 report by the Independent Sectori found that over 90% of the people who gave to charitable causes, gave to the very organizations where they volunteered. The report added:

> Households that give to and volunteer at religious congregations give an annual average of $3,164, the highest of the giving and volunteering combinations examined... In all three volunteer groups—volunteers to both religious congregations and secular organizations, volunteers to religion only, and volunteers to secular organizations only—those households that reported family involvement in volunteering **give more** than those that did not report family involvement (emphasis added).

Their conclusion was that people are far more likely to give to an organization with which they've personally worked. Why? Because they develop a sense of personal connection to both the staff as well as the clients. The lesson is clear: do whatever you can do to get as many people as possible involved in a meaningful way with your nonprofit's activities. Think of participatory events as a first step toward growing future major donors of time, materials, PR, and money.

If you have strong relationships with people who understand what you do, believe it's valuable, and enjoy participating at some level with your organization, some money will definitely come and there's lots of potential for far larger donations. But the big bucks only come after a big (and ongoing) effort to **court and support your donors**. Who makes that effort? You do. Don't worry; it's actually everyone's responsibility to help with this.

Relationships can be built every time the phone rings, the door opens, or an email arrives. You and your co-workers (at every level) should consider every conversation you have to be an opportunity to share your organization's vision, mission, values, goals, and latest project.

Note that money wasn't mentioned in that last sentence. That's because you should realize that, like your bank account, you can't make a withdrawal (plea for cash) until you've made several deposits (giving others your time and attention). Entire books and classes are dedicated to explaining ways to identify and woo new donors as well as how to get more out of existing donors. This brings us to our next topic:

Why is all of this donor relations material here in a grant-writing text? It is because the skills of fundraising must also infuse grant writing if that effort is to be successful. After all, foundations are composed of human beings who also have a substantial amount of money to distribute. The more the grant writer bears this in mind, the more likely the effort is to be well received.

This true anecdote drives the point home: A board member of an nonprofit quickly and bluntly discovered how the game is played. He accepted the job of calling potential donors (a job he enjoyed and excelled at) to solicit significant donations of money, materials, and public support. After a few calls with mixed success, one person he called briefly and accurately explained the situation:

> *"You're calling me because I have money, power, and fame and you need all three. I'm busy and don't have time to work around your schedule. If you want to talk with me further, arrange an appointment with my secretary, and I'll give you half an hour. Bring me all the information you can, let me get to know who you are, and I'll think about it."*

No doubt, this person had been called by every nonprofit in the county who knew about him. Like everyone else, wealthy people want to be treated with respect as well as sincere interest and appreciation.

Follow-up:

Pick one day for prepping, asking, and thanking

If you don't dedicate time to creating and growing relationships with people [individuals as well as groups of people like business clubs), you'll never get around to it, and only a few donors/volunteers will get the attention they deserve. The manager of an nonprofit recently wrote an article in Grassroots Fundraising magazine on this topic. They had fallen into such a bad habit of putting out fires that their donors were being ignored and, as a result, donations were down. After trying a variety of solutions, they finally found what worked best for them: dedicate one entire day to finding new donors, caring for existing donors, and personally thanking people for their contributions of time, goods, services, and cash.

For their nonprofit, Tuesday turned out to be the best day. Every Tuesday of every week was dedicated to fundraising, and everybody in the office participated. They locked the front door, closed the blinds, didn't answer the phone, ignored emails, and scheduling meetings in or out of the office was absolutely forbidden. This was a fundamental cultural change, which took time for everyone concerned to adjust to, but the rewards were well worth the effort. People could focus on one task without being distracted or feeling guilty. As a result, employees were more productive and avoided burnout, donors felt more involved as well as appreciated due to regular contacts, and fundraising projects were completed sooner and with fewer forgotten details.

For your organization, regular fundraising efforts result in regular funding contributions. This concept can be compared to filling your car's tank with gas. Rather than filling up once a year (e.g. December) and hoping you'll have enough to last, you fill up once a week (give or take). **Similarly, having regular gifts gives you stability all year round.**

Collaboration:
Working with others who share your dream

You can't do it all, but by working with other like-minded groups, you can do a lot more than you imagined. This is putting into action the age-old advice to "work smarter, not harder." Collaborating also opens you up to meeting new, and potentially future, volunteers and donors. Remember, you're networking, sharing, and cooperating; you are NOT stealing sheep!

Additionally, foundations love funding collaborations. Why? For a couple of reasons. First of all, by being part of a collaboration, you demonstrate your ability to work with others, which is key to long-term, large-scale success; this ability gives them greater confidence in your nonprofit. Second, by funding collaboration, the foundation is essentially killing two (or more) birds with one stone. Keep in mind that foundations like to tell the world all the wonderful things they're doing; many companies use their corporate foundations as a way to get free positive publicity.

Perhaps you're thinking, "That's nice, but how do I become part of a collaborative effort?" That's a good question with an easy answer: it depends. Here's another case where you'll have to ask yourself lots of questions about yourself and your nonprofit. For instance, what are your nonprofit's expertise, and your area of greatest experience? In other words, what do you bring to the table? Answering this will help you explain to other Executive Directors why they would want to collaborate with you. Also, what are issues related to, but not a part of, the issue(s) you're trying to directly address?

Let's create a working example of all these thoughts. Let's say you're working to help teenagers develop mentally, physically, spiritually, and socially. And let's say that you or one of your staff has a degree in (child) psychology, sociology, or criminal justice. Now let's say that you want to formalize and expand an after-school program for the teenagers.

You could collaborate with…

> The local animal pound so that some of the kids could help care for the facilities and animals. You'll need a vehicle and a volunteer to drive the kids there and help supervise them.

> Habitat for Humanity to get some of the kids helping build

houses or help around the office. Add another volunteer and vehicle.

Local law enforcement to have officers deliver monthly presentations on issues like gangs, graffiti, DUIs, and other issues affecting teens.

Local business clubs and unions to obtain guest speakers once a week/month to talk with the kids about the importance of education, hard work, and commitment. This might lead to a Junior Achievement or job training program.

The city and the local garden club to start a veggie and flower garden designed by and cared for by the teens. That's a 2-for-1 deal!

Documentation:

Statistics and Benchmarking

Are you doing a good job? Can you prove it? How would you prove it? You prove it with statistics and you get statistics by benchmarking the most important aspects of your nonprofit, its programs, and the issues those programs address.

People, and especially foundations, will help you only if you can prove a problem exists and you're doing a great job to fix it. As helpful as recommendations are, they tend to be oriented around feelings, emotions, and hunches: "I just love YOUR nonprofit. They've been so nice to me over the years and really helped me get my life back on track. I can't tell you how much they've changed my life."

Well, they're certainly right on that last point because they haven't been tracking exactly what you've done for them, how that's changed their life, and to what extent. When was the last time you heard a client say:

> "YOUR nonprofit has significantly impacted my life in a variety of areas. Over the past 18 months, they've helped me decrease my alcohol consumption by 90%, eliminate my recreational drug use, and provided me job training skills which enabled me to get a new job making 37% more net income per month. Because of all this I'm a happier person, sleep better at night, and have a more enjoyable relationship with my spouse. Thank you so much!"

Yeah, right, dream on. But those are the kind of numbers that foundations want to see, so you have to generate the statistics for yourself. Numbers can help balance the touchy-feely quotes. At this point, someone is bound to be thinking, "Our goal is to change people's lives. You can't measure that." Well, yes and no. Obviously, you can't attach a machine to them as if you were checking their heart rate. But you can create a survey that would help you and them begin to concretely identify the critical goals your program is trying to address.

Don't assume your nonprofit and its programs can't be benchmarked, and if you're not a numbers person, find someone who's willing to spend the time to generate the documentation necessary for your success.

Here are some examples of information you might want to track about your clients:

- New or repeat client
- Gender
- Race
- Age: child, teen, adult, senior
- Number of referrals made to other agencies/ministries
- Number of people referred to you by other agencies/ministries

Consider using a computerized database so you can "check" people in as the first step of your program. Remember, you're not trying to be nosy, just trying to identify your average client. You should also consider tracking the number of referrals you make to other programs as well as how many people are referred to you and by whom. Regardless of your history or current circumstances, never exaggerate your numbers; individual donors as well as foundations respect accuracy.

Here's how numbers can help you. Suppose you discover that the majority of your clients are single mothers. That would easily qualify you for foundations as well as government agencies that focus on women and children. Or perhaps 75% of the participants in your weekend basketball league are teens; this would lead you to seek funding for youth development, educational, health, or crime prevention programs.

Naysayers:
Addressing and Minimizing Their Impact

No matter who you are or what you're doing, somebody somewhere at some time will have something negative to say about you personally, your nonprofit in general, and/or one of your nonprofit's programs or staff. They might have a good point; they might not. Either way, you need to look into the matter to determine the situation and what, if any, corrective action is necessary.

In today's lawsuit-crazy world, maintaining proper and complete documentation is now considered as critical as paying the power bill – you couldn't operate without it. Sometimes you can answer somebody by saying, "We've done a background check and they met our requirements," or, "All the financial records are in order and have been independently audited and confirmed; here's a copy."

Other times the bad feelings are a result of poor communication. Maybe you didn't use the right words; maybe they were paying more attention to rumors than what you told them. In any case, you'll have to decide if the issue is worth your time and if the person has a significant chance of harming you, your nonprofit, or your staff.

In the category of "easier said than done," try to be as proactive as possible. Keep an ear out for anything that you think could become an issue in the future. Try to address it before anyone else does. Let other people help you identify what anyone could possibly have against you, and then do your best to address the issue and put a positive spin on whatever you can. Unfortunately, we don't have any quick and easy answers for you. And based on our years of experience, you have our encouragement and sympathies.

Grant Writing Leadership

This text is largely devoted to the production of grant proposals. But of equal importance with the sound research, good writing, and the other elements of successful grant writing; is YOUR LEADERSHIP of this part of the full set of your organization's development strategies. A leader-less grant proposal writing project is not likely to result in success in the highly competitive environment of grant seeking. Here are some considerations for your leadership and action when you approach grants as a funding source.

Consultant Performance Expectations. Organizations whose resources permit the hiring of professional grant writers rightly concentrate proposal development on such professionals. It is important for there to be clarity of the organizations' expectations. The job description for a grant writer should include expectations regarding the production of proposals – and not on dollar values of grants awarded. Remember that grant seeking is highly competitive and even the best efforts a good writer may not be funded.

Compensation. Some organizations may be tempted to offer compensation to a grant writer on a results-based formula. As logical as this may seem, this practice violates the most widely accepted canon of ethics in fundraising, the Code of Ethical Principles and Standards of the Association of Fundraising Professionals. The code notes that such professionals "shall not accept compensation or enter into a contract that is based on a percentage of contributions; nor shall members accept finder's fees or contingent fees."ii

If your organization hires a grant writer or contracts this function to a professional firm, it should be done on a "compensation related to work performed" basis.

The compensation package; however, may be established with an expectation of its pay being supplemented with some form of bonus (as provided for in the same Code of Ethics):

> "Members may accept performance-based compensation, such as bonuses, provided such bonuses are in accord with prevailing practices within the members' own organizations and are not based on a percentage of contributions."

Read this code at: http://www.afpnet.org/Ethics/EnforcementDetail. cfm?ItemNumber=3261.

First actions – are yours! In the following text, we strongly recommend that the first piece of a grant proposal development effort is the budget for the program to be funded, as well as for the organization as a whole. It is not likely that a grant writer would have the capacity to address this task apart from the organization's fiscal personnel, so before the writer is assigned the task of seeking funding, the budget preparation needs to be completed.

Doing it in-house? Newer and smaller nonprofit and ministries will not be in a position to hire a grant writer. These groups must rely upon a team of staff members and/or volunteers to carry out a grant writing strategy. While this effort is not likely to be "tidy", it has the potential to energize the entire organization.

There are several steps to the initiation of this approach and to keeping the effort on track and productive.

> 1. Recruit volunteers to join in this effort. These volunteers must be encouraged to approach the task with an open mind and a willingness to think "outside the box."

> 2. Energize the team! One of the great struggles in the not-for-profit sector is the lack of funds to meet the needs of the organizations themselves and/or the needs of the people they serve. This lack of funding easily breeds discouragement and a lowering of expectations in pursuit of the organizations' visions. Energize the team with the message that there is funding available for nearly any

need, and that it can be obtained by following the best practices of grant research and proposal preparation. Current lack of funding for a program or project need not be a barrier to growth, but rather the impetus to get busy.

3. Establish funding priorities. This is both a beginning step and an ongoing process. The team should meet regularly to establish funding priorities and to ensure that the efforts to meet those priorities are on track. Input from everyone involved in the organization should be welcomed, but it is the team's job to prioritize the funding requests.

4. Delegate responsibilities among the team. Some people will perform well at researching funding sources, some at the research to substantiate a funding need, others at the actual composition of proposals.

5. Establish timelines for completion. Most foundations and government funding opportunities have clearly stated due dates for proposals. These must be taken into consideration and the team's timelines should be established to provide a "cushion" in order to be certain that proposal submissions are made on time.

Grant proposal process management. While the grant application and proposal process can be managed by either a volunteer or staff member, this person should be well versed in the entirety of the grant writing process. The leader/convener should also be facile with motivating and inspiring others because it is easy for people to become frustrated and discouraged in the process of grant writing and in light of the reality that "no" is a more common response to a grant proposal than is "yes". Refer to Step 2, above, as an ongoing and purposeful step to keep the team engaged. The leader of the grant writing team need not be involved in any particular piece of the whole process, but must be conversant with the totality of the effort.

In the final analysis, the leadership board and the executive director must be fully supportive the grant writing agenda whether that is carried out by professional staff, program staff, or volunteers. Before embarking on any course of grant writing, it is essential that these key leaders of the organization select an approach and support those who carry it out.

Introduction to Grant Writing

WHAT is a grant?

According to Merriam – Webster, a grant is "something granted; especially: a gift (as of land or money) for a <u>particular purpose</u>."

In the nonprofit and philanthropic sectors, a grant is usually monetary, given by a funder for their particular purpose, is most often awarded through a competitive process, and once given, becomes a contracted transactional relationship between the granting organization and the performing organization – in its simplest terms, money given to support performance delivered.

More to the point for your organization or ministry, a grant is the award of money to support a program or project that you also want, or even feel called, to carry out (your vision) – and that falls within the granting organization's felt burden for support (their vision).

As you will see, grants are not free money for you to do with as you please. They are the result of a very deliberate process by which you do some or all of the following:

- Identify an unmet need or a problem in your organization or in the community you serve
- Design or adopt a solution whose outcome will resolve that problem or need
- Discover sources of funding who share your concern about the problem or need and who seek outcomes consistent with those you seek
- Prepare an organized proposal for funding
- Submit your proposal -- on the funder's schedule and in the funder's format

The purpose of this text is to examine the grant writing process in order to be successful in acquiring grant funding. Much of what we will address is work that must be in place before sitting down to the keyboard. It is hoped that each step will be followed carefully.

One of the key organizations in the United States for grant writing is the Foundation Directory. More and more, the process we will describe is what they refer to as "grant seeking." It is a great deal more than writing!

WHO can get a grant?

Almost any person or group can get a grant. Not all grants, however, come from the same source. Just as each non-profit has its own vision or mission, foundations have unique, selected giving areas. Knowing these specifications can tell you up front whether or not you should bother requesting funds from them. Some foundations, for example, give only to nonprofits who have an IRS 501(c)3 determination. Others give to private companies or to individual people. The same differences are true of government funding.

Among the foundations that limit giving to 501(c)3 groups, you will find further specifications as far as what types of groups they will and will not give to. For example, some will fund religious organizations while others specify only Catholic programs. Other foundations prefer to fund education, the arts, or medical research. Foundations may limit their giving to a specific city, such as Dallas, TX, county (Fort Worth), or state (Texas). Others are regional (giving only in the Pacific North West for example), while others give on a national or even international basis. Some foundations also limit their giving to specific age groups, gender, or background. For example, one foundation may focus on teen moms and battered women, while another funds programs for the blind or physically disabled.

Foundations typically specify what type of expenses they're willing to fund as well. Some will fund specific things, such as school buses, equipment, or computers. Others will contribute to salaries, special events, or construction. Similarly, you will find foundations that choose NOT to fund certain things (one example might be a private foundation that funds general expenses but not building projects). Here are some terms a foundation might use to describe what they will or will not support:

annual campaigns • building/renovation funds • capital support challenge grants • conferences and seminars • consulting services continuing support or continuation grant • employee matching gifts endowments fellowships • general operating expenses matching funds • program development • research • scholarships seed money • technical assistance

Most of the people we work with can narrow their search down to foundations who will fund 501(c)3 organizations as well as their area of interest. Most of our clients need funding to pay for things and salaries.

WHAT kinds of grantors are out there?

You can find grants from private foundations or companies, corporations, the government, and even from other nonprofits. Typically, private foundations were originally founded (and funded) by a wealthy person or family as an opportunity for them to give back to the community.

Private and public companies often create foundations to build good public relations (PR). This may sound cynical, but it is the bottom line.

In fact, many large companies have two giving programs: the "XYZ Corp. Foundation" in addition to a separate "XYZ Corp. Community Giving Program" which is NOT technically a foundation and does not have to follow the laws laid out for a foundation. Basically, the corporate foundation operates independently of the company and has a vision/mission that is separate from the actual company supporting it. The foundation's mission typically reflects what their parent company's clients expect to see from them. The giving program, however, is part of the company itself and operates accordingly. Such programs are often managed by someone in the company's marketing department and used to fund whatever will generate the best PR.

So what does this mean for you? The main thing to remember is that, as a non-profit, you can apply for funding from a corporate foundation as can anyone else on their announcement of requests for proposals (RFP).

On the other hand, in order to apply for a grant from the giving program you must be willing to invest more time in building relationships. This may start with knowing someone within the company who has the ability to sell the company on your program through a winning pitch. If you can collaborate with someone on "the inside," you may get your foot in the door to ask for a grant later.

For example, let's say your organization helps women who are making a new start after leaving an abusive relationship. You know someone in a corporation who works with you and eventually arranges for a specific number of your most promising clients to receive employment and advanced training. Everything works out well and your clients do a great job. This program enables you to build relationships as well as good PR for them as word spreads of how they helped these struggling women rebuild their lives. A year or so later you take someone from the corporation on a tour of your organization's shelter, which stimulates conversation about other needs within your organization that this particular organization might be able to help with. The more they help and support with funds the more you spread the word about them. They recognize the win-win situation and support you through their corporate giving program.

Yes, this process takes awhile, but it's a way that benefits you greatly in the long run.

Federal, state, and local governments support nonprofit service providers because it is more efficient to fund such providers than for the government to create and operate a program. It is critical for a nonprofit to develop alertness for government funds when they become available.

HOW much should you request?

More detail will follow regarding researching foundations, but the determination of how much to ask for is an important element to be resolved by research. Some foundations and corporate funding programs, as well as all government grants will provide limits and, often, ranges to guide your request.

If a listing, a website, or an RFP does not provide such information, it is relatively simple to find. Foundations are required to make their IRS Form 990 available to the public. On that form, there is a listing of every beneficiary of the foundation's resources for a given tax year.

If, in review of a foundation's giving, you learn that their maximum gift in the previous year was $20,000, they are not likely to respond favorably to your request for $100,000.

It is also helpful to compare your organization in size, scope and budget history with the organization the foundation funded last year.

WHEN should you apply?

Each foundation is different. With most, you can apply one time per year. One process might allow you to reapply. Let's say a foundation turns down your request for funding. You can call them and ask for a follow-up interview to learn why your program was not accepted. Was something lacking in your proposal? Is it possible for you to resubmit your proposal according to what you have learned? You may still have to wait a full year to resubmit but this time you will know what they are looking for.

Some foundations and government agencies will allow organizations to create an "addendum" and attach it to the same proposal. You then submit the same proposal that you sent before with the new addendum attached.

With some foundations, you can apply more than once per year as long as it's for a different program or need. For example, you submit a proposal in January asking for contributions to a building project. Six months later, you call on the same foundation for funding to cover computer equipment. In August you request funds for salaries and in December send a proposal for general operating expenses. It's unlikely that you'll return to the same foundation this many times in one year, but in rare cases, it is possible as long as each proposal is clearly covering a new need.

Another great way to add flexibility to your grant writing process is to break your program into multiple phases. This allows you to ask the same foundation to fund the same type of request for each phase. Note that you will only ask for one phase at a time.

Timing is crucial when it comes to applying for grants. Government grants are often given in cycles or "funding rounds." This means that you may only apply during specified months of the year. Be sure to research and know the deadlines so you don't miss them. Stay in touch with your contacts at all levels. You don't want to put off you opportunity to apply until the next year!

WHY bother with all the red tape?

It's worth your time and energy to pay attention to details. There is a great deal of money available to you and you don't want to miss out on opportunities due to laziness or a need to rush. Remember foundations are required BY LAW to give away 5% of their money each year. Actually, they must average 5% over a 3-year period so it serves them well to give more now and then.

Again, this giving is a MUST. So they need to give as much as you need to receive. They exist to give money away. But you aren't the only one who needs it. The competition is greater than ever.

Why?

- There are more non-profit organizations than ever before.
- More non-profits have learned about foundations and grants.
- Foundations have more money to give away than they used to.

This is not a reason for being intimidated. Rather, it is a great opportunity. If you are willing to do the work required to submit a winning proposal then you have what it takes to get a foundation's attention.

It all comes down to quality — quality presented in just the right way. Send a well prepared proposal to several of the right foundations and you may earn your program $100,000 or more per year.

WHERE do grantors exist and WHO will they fund?

Both private and corporate foundations exist in almost every county in the United States. They are, however, much more common in cities. Over the past 100 years, Americans have moved out of the rural communities into larger cities and towns. Foundations have followed their lead. Consequently, their money went with them to converge on major towns and cities. Since foundations are often created thanks to a wealthy family or company, the foundations are created where wealthy people tend to live.

Foundations also fund non-profits located in cities far more often than they do rural groups.

Let's say you grew up in Boston Mass, graduated from Yale, worked for 20 years in San Francisco, and finally retired in Reno, NV. After buying a spacious house, a car or two and every tool or "toy" you ever wanted, you realize that you have an extra $50 million burning a hole in your bank accounts. What to do? You have always wanted to help those in need. And then there are the obvious tax benefits of charitable giving. You decide to create the "I.M. Nota Miser Foundation." After much consideration, you decide to focus on education. For the sake of pure convenience, you'll probably form and base your foundation in your current hometown. You might also choose to have your foundation primarily funds non-profits located in or serving the communities of MA, communities surrounding Yale University, and the San Francisco Bay Area, as well as the state of Nevada. On paper, this might look like an odd grouping of service areas. In reality, you are serving the communities that you know and care about.

Remember: relationships first, money second.

In the end, your chances of getting a foundation's support are better if:

- You develop and maintain strong relationships within your community
- Live near a major city
- Generate positive media for yourself and your donors

Myth Busting for Nonprofits

Myth #1 - Foundations never fund religious organizations.

It's true that certain foundations choose not to support religious groups. That is their prerogative and is not true of all foundations. Many prefer to support church-run or religious programs. Others are not concerned about religion as long as the program is strong and it fits within their guidelines.

Myth #2 - Only well-known nonprofits like Big Brothers, Big Sisters get funding.

Size has nothing to do with whether or not a program will find funding.

Well-known programs may receive a larger cut of the donations, but only because they've been around long enough to know exactly what to ask for and how. These larger nonprofits often have the advantage of a full-time employee who does nothing but look for funding and writing grant proposals. Smaller groups simply have more homework to do.

Cautions before you begin

Have realistic expectations. A successful grant proposal might bring 25-50% of what you originally asked for. It's rare to get all that you want. Like you, foundations have budgets and can only give away predetermined amounts of money. In addition to this, most foundations understand that organizations will ask for more than they really need.

Some grants come with firm restrictions. All grants come with some restrictions. For example, a foundation may give you $10 million to build a new youth center, with the condition that you only spend it on new construction. This means that you can't set part of it aside to make repairs on your existing facility or pull part of the award for salaries. With this in mind you need to develop a complete funding plan that will cover startup, new projects, as well as ongoing expenses.

Finally, pay attention to details. Some might seem superficial but can make a big difference to a foundation. If you are sending to a non-religious foundation but your organization is connected to a church, you'll want to avoid religious lingo in your cover letter and proposal. If you are submitting a proposal for a city beautification project, make sure you use recycled paper. What might make your proposal stand out in a good way OR a negative way?

How Do You Get Where You Need to Be?

Funders, private, corporate, and governmental, want to fund organizations that "have their acts together". They must be certain that their money will not be used for private gain but for public benefit. There are several ways to operate in the "nonprofit sector" and it is the organization's responsibility to decide what kind of organization it is to be and to structure itself appropriately, according to type.

Should you be a 501(c)3 or a "DBA"?
There are many options as far as how to set up your organization and each has pros and cons. This is a good time for you to sit down with those

you know who run non-profit programs. How are they organized? Why did they choose this route? Ask them to share stories. Listen carefully and take notes.

Here are three common options:

501(c)3

This is how most non-profits, including churches, are organized. Most choose this for the tax benefits. 501(c)3 organizations are tax exempt. Your donors benefit by a tax deduction for each donation that they send to you. One of the requirements for a 501(c)3 is that you must have a board of directors to make the major decision. This means finding a group of people that you trust with decisions that might make or break your program. While many federal grant opportunities are open to organizations that do not have this status, most foundations do require it to be eligible for funding.

"DBA" or Doing Business As

This can be the fastest way to get your program started. You can start by choosing an original name and operating under a pre-existing non-profit. Individuals can donate to your program and get their tax deduction through your "parent" non-profit. If you operate under a church or some other program that many foundations choose not to fund, however, you may have trouble when it comes time to send grant proposals. But you can always turn your nonprofit into a 501(c)3 once your program is off the ground.

Private Company

Whether this is a Sole Proprietorship or a Limited Liability Corporation, this is an option for those who don't want to answer to a board of directors. However, your donors will not receive tax benefits for funding your program. On top of that, you will pay taxes on any profit that your company takes in. But maybe your company is your outreach. In that case, the Private Company route is for you. Just remember that you'll be relying on sales of your products and/or services when it comes to making money for your company.

Building Relationships

This isn't as difficult as it sounds. But it does take a lot of time, effort, and emotion. If you can't afford to hire someone to oversee all of your fundraising, then either you or one of your volunteers will need to take this on. Someone in your organization should be spending an average of 8 hours per week on building relationships. That's one full working day.

You or your volunteer can expect to spend time doing the following:

- **Contact your major donors and volunteers via phone calls,** e-mails, or postal mail. Some form of personal communication is needed and always appreciated. Face it, we all like quality time and attention. But there must also be a purpose behind such contacts. It should be more than a way to kill time so you have something to check off your list at the end of the day.

- **Meet people in person for the purpose of sharing your vision with them**. Newsletters are great. Hopefully everyone in your organization is sharing your vision with those they know. But nobody can communicate your passion like you can. After all, you are the one who originally caught it. Good communication and a professional appearance will only help. The key though, is a sincere approach. Share your vision and passion with others and the weak moments in your "presentation" will slip from their minds.

- **Write thank you notes.** Did someone go out of their way for you or your program? Thank the person. Do this after lunch meetings as well. Let anyone who took time out of their schedule for you know that you appreciated it. Handwritten letters and envelopes add a personal touch. You want them to know that you, Mike Stickler, appreciate them, Charles White, and their specific action – rather than "Dear Donor." Use a real stamp so it will stand out from junk mail and bills.

- **Write articles for your newsletter.** Your newsletter should stand out in a good way when recipients find it in their mail. It should have a unique look with content that is more than the typical rehashed fluff or statistics. Keep articles short but captivating. Use bullet points, photos, graphs, and other visuals to illustrate your point and draw the reader in.

- **Update your database of donors and volunteers.** No matter how nice your newsletter is, it will mean nothing if it arrives at the wrong address.

Choose a "people person" to do the above jobs. If the thought of writing notes and calling people doesn't thrill you, find someone who does enjoy it. Your program will live and die by the relationships holding it together.

Paperwork

Create a file drawer and label it "Documents for Grant Writing" or some recognizable abbreviation for this. You may not need all the items for any one proposal but you will need each of them at some point. Better to have everything in place now to avoid a last minute panic in the future.

Required Documents to Submit With Applications

- Your Vision and Mission Statements
- Copy of State Articles of Incorporation
- Long Range Plan
- Current (dated) Board of Directors with bios & photos (passport type is fine) including principles, board members, and staff
- Most recent audit or financial review (note that a full-blown audit can cost $7,500+ and may not be necessary)
- Most Recent IRS Form 990 or 990EZ
- Annual Operating Budget (current)
- 501 (c)3 Determination Letter

Documents to have Available for Request

- Board Minutes (at least for the last 12 months)
- Board Orientation Packet, Manual, or Job Descriptions
- Board Training Materials
- Policies on Conflicts of Interest, Nepotism & Code of Ethics
- Bylaws or Other Authorizing Documents
- Financial Policies and Procedures
- Accreditation Documents, if possible
- Applicable Licenses
- Needs Assessment
- Records Management Policies
- Evidence of Collaboration
- Program Evaluation Documents
- Job Descriptions for both staff and volunteers
- Personnel Policies
- Equal Employment Opportunity (EEO) policies
- Wage and Salary Plan for paid staff
- Code of Ethics
- Documentation of Training Programs for Staff
- Evidence of Facility Insurance
- Fire Inspection Reports
- OSHA Inspection Reports, if applicable

How to Get a Grant

You may have heard:

> *Getting grants is so easy. I used to do it for a living. You just call a few foundations, fill out their forms, send them in, and boom; they send you a check!*

We've heard it too, usually from people who worked for major public organizations with full marketing departments, a strong reputation for high-profile service in their community, and long-standing relationships under their belts. It's easy for the programs that most foundations already know about and can count on for good PR in exchange for their investment. These organizations may even get away with sending proposals full of holes. You see, foundations are similar to your average donor – they want to fund winners. They want to feel good about the checks they write.

Chances are that you don't have a decades-long relationship with numerous foundations. That takes years (well, decades) to build up. We aren't saying this to discourage you. We simply want you to approach grant writing with a realistic idea of the work involved. But don't panic! There is hope for even the smallest non-profit.

Please approach grant writing with patience! Preparation takes time. Research takes time. And grant-makers rarely operate "on demand." Foundations, corporate giving programs, and government agencies issue grants on their timetable, not on yours.

Grant Mechanics

Before any writing of a grant proposal begins, the writer or team must fully understand any requirements the foundation or agency to whom you will be submitting. Foundations may issue an RFP for a particular funding opportunity or, more often, they will issue a set of grant guidelines, which are to be followed by all applicants. Government funding sources will issue an RFP, a NOFA, or an SGA, which will provide similar information.

It is incumbent on the grant writer or grant team to be familiar with each detail of these documents. Among the issues addressed will be instructions regarding margins, types of paper (a certain weight, color or a requirement to use recycled paper, etc.), the order of assembly of the proposal package, the number of copies to be submitted, page limits and grant qualifications. Ignoring or overlooking these instructions and guidelines will result in a rejected proposal. It cannot be emphasized enough that failure to follow guidelines will meant that no matter how well prepared, how diligently planned, and how carefully documented your proposal may be, it will not be funded.

Guidelines such as we have described are not merely arbitrary. The make it possible for the foundations and the government to more easily review the proposals submitted. The proposal you submit will be reviewed by a human being who should not have to figure out how each proposal is formatted in order to measure one against the other fairly.

Here and in the more detailed discussion of the grant proposal by section, the information is arranged in the order by which a proposal would normally be submitted. There are distinctive purposes to each section of a successful proposal. The order in which the individual sections are completed is not the order in which the material is submitted to the funder.

It might be said that the preparation of a proposal is an organic rather than a linear process, because the work that goes into one section will inform the development of one or more of the other sections of the final proposal.

Example of Organization of a Submitted Proposal

- Cover Letter
- Application form if the foundation requires one
- Foundation Specific Form(s)
- Summary
- Introduction
- Problem Statement or Needs Assessment
- Objective(s)
- Methods and Case Studies
- Evaluation
- Future or Other Necessary Funding
- Budget

Recommended Order for Preparation of the Proposal

- Identify the problem or need to be addressed
- Develop a plan, program, or project to address the identified need or problem
- Prepare a detailed and justified budget
- Write the organizational introduction
- Prepare the statement of objectives
- Develop and detail the methods to be employed
- Structure the evaluation of the project being funded
- Describe plans for future funding of ongoing program
- Prepare the abstract or Executive Summary
- Application or other foundation-specific forms as required
- Cover Letter and/or LOI

What You Should Know About Funding

In order to craft a proposal that will get the attention you desire you need to learn about the foundations that you are contacting. This will help you learn their requirements and gain understanding of their funding priorities. Some foundations exist to support a single cause. Detailed research will reveal this information. Small foundations, for example, rarely fund unsolicited ("cold call") proposals (those that just arrive in the mail without a phone call or letter of inquiry preceding it). Personal contact and established integrity on the part of the applicant is very important to the reviewers and the foundation Board, because by comparison to large foundations, they often have less money to give away. Larger foundations also often establish a predetermined list of organizations that they choose to fund so getting your foot in the door is difficult without some kind of referral or personal contact. So in most cases "cold call" proposals are not productive.

A quality proposal is crucial for both the small and the large foundations. Smaller funding sources see an unknown organization as a gamble. Larger ones are unlikely to fund anyone without a clear-cut plan that will clearly benefit the community. So you can't afford to slack off when contacting any potential donors. This relates both to the quality of your presentation and to its content. It is nearly futile to submit presentations that have not been prepared with all of the attention a good proposal demands.

A similar, but distinct, source of funding is the "corporate responsibility" division of many large corporations. These funding opportunities are often targeted to localities in which the company in question operates. The relationship to foundation funding is that the approach and the proposal are very alike, and require the same due diligence of research. To locate these sources, research the major corporations headquartered or that have a branch in your locale. Most will have a website that can be researched regarding corporate giving.

Format

Our format is not the answer to all your funding problems. It is just a clear-cut way of organizing your program and current needs. Use this format to map out your plans then use it as a sort of template when it comes time to contact specific foundations.

Private Foundations:
When applying to a foundation or corporation, you will almost always need to send a letter outlining who you are, why you exist, and the

amount of money you are requesting. This letter is often referred to as a Letter of Intent (LOI). Use this format to structure your letter:

Limit yourself to three pages or less. Be sure to address all areas that the foundation has specific requirements or preferences on. This letter should be signed by the chief executive officer, executive director, or president of your organization and should be accompanied by a cover letter signed by the chairperson of your organization's board of directors. In addition, the foundation may request:

- A copy of your total annual budget for the past year or two
- An audited financial statement or 990
- Your IRS letter of determination (if you are a nonprofit organization)
- Letters of support
- An annual (or comparable) report, if you have one

Government Funding Sources:

While few foundations or corporations require special grant application forms, the Government typically does. Follow their instructions carefully. Do not consider our format a substitute for any specific directions. If you don't understand the instructions, call and ask for clarification. Many government organizations use score sheets and assign points to different components of each proposal that comes in. If you can, request a copy of the grading scale. This will help you along as you prepare your application and proposal.

Proposal Writing Basics

1. Make Your Proposal Neat, Clean and Readable

Do a thorough check for spelling and grammar errors and typos. Unless the foundation requests more (and they often do, so be sure to check), send one copy of the proposal. Break up the proposal text with headings (for example "Our History," "Current Needs" "Tracking Success"). A page of unbroken print is hard on the eyes. Keep your focus on the proposal content, not on costly covers and fancy fonts. If you stray from the norm, do it well.

2. Speak English

Proposal writing is not an opportunity to display your vast knowledge of language. No need to break out the thesaurus. Avoid jargon even if the foundation uses it in their guidelines, unless you feel you absolutely must use some. Those reviewing your proposal might not be fluent in it. To test the clarity of your writing, have friends or family read your proposal. Some of your best comments will come from people who know nothing about your program. If they don't get it, the reviewer might not either.

3. Keep it Short

What is the proper length for a proposal? Just long enough for you to clearly communicate your message, but not long enough to put your reader to sleep.

"I have made this letter longer than usual, only because I have not had time to make it shorter."
- Blaise Pascal, 17th-century French philosopher and mathematician, (often misattributed to Mark Twain)

4. Be Positive

Take your grant personally, when it comes to how you approach writing it. Get excited about the program so your reader will get excited. Think of this as a chance to offer a foundation the chance to take part in something great—something important that will change lives forever. This isn't begging for money. There is no need to apologize for yourself or your request. Keep in mind that foundations benefit too. They want to fund winning programs so show them that you are one. Leave out confessions of past mistakes and program failures. Don't say something like:

"We are sure that you are aware of the sudden disappearance of our organization's founder and the questions surrounding his past conduct. Be assured that this is in no way a reflection of our values as an organization. We have made great strides since that time to rebuild our board and have seen some promising new leaders rise up and do an even better job. I truly believe that our program is stronger than ever before, in spite of this temporary setback."

This is a time to stress your strengths!

5. Avoid Unsupported Information

These are easy to spot for the experienced reader. Unsupported assumptions include:

*   Leaving out key information about your organization as if the reader already knows your history, purpose, and affiliations.

*   Citing the gravity of a problem without backing it up with statistics, quotes, and other references.

*   Citing events that have little or nothing to do with your needs in hopes that donors will see some kind of connection.

*   Using "We believe" or "We have observed" in place of real facts.

The examples are endless. Obviously, you don't want to overload the potential donor with statistics, facts, graphs, and charts either. Give just enough evidence to support your point. But do support it with solid evidence. Cite sources of such information in the body of the proposal rather than adding footnotes. Remember, you're not writing a term paper.

The Grant Proposal – By Section

A private foundation and a government department will, in an announcement document, or the grant guidelines, provide instruction as to the order in which the individual parts of the proposal are to be submitted. One of the biggest mistakes a beginning grant writer can make is to prepare the proposal in the order set for submission.

In the budget section which follows, one should not imagine that because the budget will likely be examined first it should be completed first. In fact, the budget will need to be prepared as the need or problem to be addressed is identified; and a program is planned to affect that solution (along with an evaluation plan created to measure that program's effectiveness).

Researching Foundations and other Grant Makers

We can't emphasize enough how important it is to find the right match for your program. You can write the slickest, most detailed grant proposal and include all the required elements and attachments, but if you send it to the wrong foundation, those polished pages won't mean a thing to them.

This research is also fundamental to achieving what grant writing is best equipped to do: provide funding outside your normal revenue streams in order to accomplish something new or improve on something that already works, but could be better or expanded.

In your research, you are looking for funding sources who provide the type of funding you seek (i.e., "general operating funds"), who operate in your geographic area, and whose ultimate purpose is in harmony with your vision and mission.

The Foundation Center publishes books and software to help you identify potential funders. Many are long and detailed. You could also visit the main branch of your town's library and check out a copy. These resources allow you to search by keywords and categories. For example, you could ask a search engine to find all foundations located in Reno, Nevada having the word "homeless" in their stated purpose.

Of course, it's also possible to reinvent this concept for yourself. Using the Foundation Center's software, for example, you can apply the same concept to grant research. If you know of a group that has programs similar to yours, you can do a search for that group's name and find out all the foundations that gave them grants. Which foundations gave repeat funding? Which gave more than a certain amount? You can then look these foundations up and read their descriptions. By doing all of this you can begin to generate a list of "keywords" so you can find other foundations with similar purpose statements more easily. You can also get an idea for what kind of funding you can expect to receive.

The best CD package lets you search by: grant maker name; state; city; grant maker type; geographic focus; establishment date; fields of interest; trustees, officers, and donors; text search; types of support; total assets; total giving; corporate name; corporate location. Specific to grants database: recipient name; recipient state; recipient city; subjects; grant amount; year authorized; and recipient type.

Most of our clients can narrow their search down to foundations willing to fund 501(c)3 organizations that have a similar background to theirs and want to improve the local community. Most of our clients need funding to pay for specific items, salaries, and general expenses.iii

Armed with all the information gathered in your research, your grant proposal can be prepared with the funders' priorities in mind as well as your own.

The following page presents a "flow chart" which shows how all of this planning must be done in an integrated way for any of your proposal to make sense. Once all of that work is done, the grant writer's job is to extract the information needed for each section that follows.

Before one word is written, it is vital to have identified the need or problem to be addressed and to compile data to substantiate that need or problem. A program or project must be defined along with the methods by which it will be carried out. The cost of all of this must be determined and income streams identified. Then, and only then, can a grant proposal be prepared.

Think of grant writing as an "organic" rather than a linear process and you will avoid most of the mistakes made by newcomers to this field.

I. The Proposal Budget

As we will see, there is a considerable amount of planning involved in creating a fundable proposal. There is a "which came first?" dynamic in play between project or program planning and the budget. We will start with consideration of the budget because **the budget is the first part of your proposal that will be reviewed.** If your budget is well done, in balance, justified, and reasonable, the rest of the proposal will have a chance. If not, the rest of your effort will go unread.

Each funding source has its own requirements when it comes to how

Flowchart of a Grant Proposal

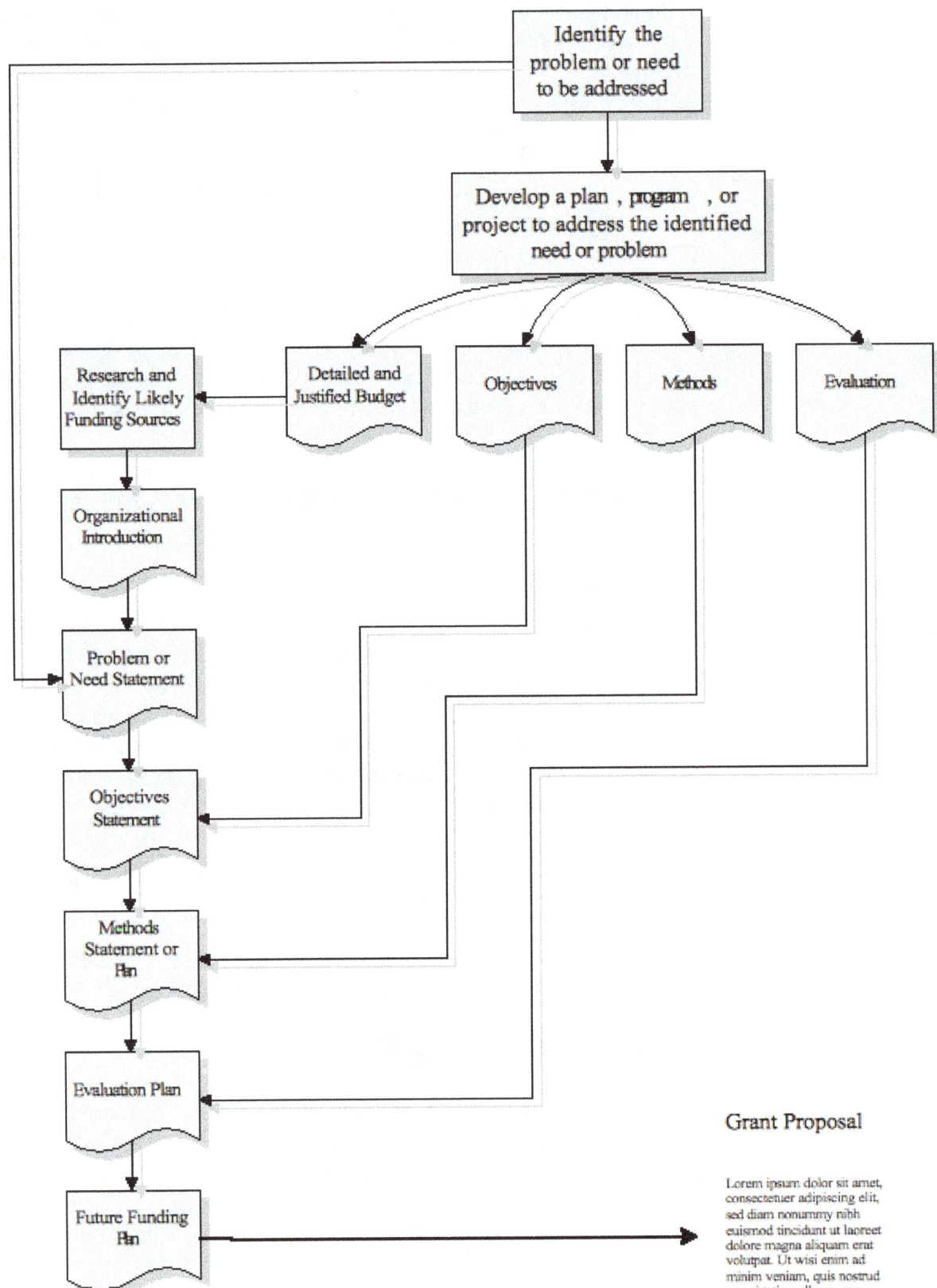

```
                                            ┌─────────────────────┐
                                            │   Identify the      │
                                            │ problem or need     │
                                            │ to be addressed     │
                                            └─────────────────────┘
                                                      │
                                                      ▼
                                            ┌─────────────────────┐
                                            │ Develop a plan , program , or │
                                            │ project to address the identified │
                                            │    need or problem  │
                                            └─────────────────────┘
```

| Research and Identify Likely Funding Sources | Detailed and Justified Budget | Objectives | Methods | Evaluation |

Organizational Introduction

Problem or Need Statement

Objectives Statement

Methods Statement or Plan

Evaluation Plan

Future Funding Plan

Grant Proposal

Lorem ipsum dolor sit amet, consectetuer adipiscing elit, sed diam nonummy nibh euismod tincidunt ut laoreet dolore magna aliquam erat volutpat. Ut wisi enim ad minim veniam, quis nostrud exerci tation ullamcorper suscipit lobortis nisl ut aliquip ex ea commodo consequat.

much detail you must include about your budget. Government funding sources usually require a lot of details, including completion of budget forms. Foundations and corporations tend to be less demanding. Still, including your budget will be appreciated and only shows your attention to detail and planning. Just as you follow individual guidelines in preparing the individual sections of your proposal, you want to adhere to instructions in the budget requirements. Whether you are required to go into this much detail or not, it's best to follow the guidelines of government organizations. Their format will force you to include all of the information that you will need available. When it comes time to prepare proposals for individual foundations, prepare the budget section according to their requirements.

"I have enough money to last me the rest of my life, unless I buy something."

–Jackie Mason

Estimating Your Budget

And it is an estimate. We rarely know exactly how much something will cost. Prices change, people raise their fees, and expenses come up without warning. Knowing this, funding sources will allow you a certain amount of leeway in how you spend your money, as long as you do not spend more than the total amount of the grant they award. It is okay if not every penny of the grant money is spent as you laid out in the budget. You have certain degrees of freedom in spending grant funds. Requests for additional changes may be authorized by the funding source (requests for changes must be submitted in writing—this is known as a formal "budget modification"). Of course, the more carefully you plan your budget, the less likely you are to require major modifications.

Getting Into Specifics

Once again, it's time to get specific. You might be tempted to round your budget to the nearest thousand and move on. All this does is tell your reviewer that you haven't taken much time in examining actual costs. If you must do some rounding, do it to the nearest hundred or ten. Avoid categories like "miscellaneous" and "contingency" Items that you see falling into these categories should be accounted for. For example, if a staff member is due for a cost-of-living raise, work that increase into the amount requested to cover salaries (in other words, look ahead). If you plan the purchase of a piece of equipment, find out how much it will cost and work it into the written budget. This level of planning will not only work in your favor when it comes time to review your proposal, but it will also benefit your program in the long run.

What Format Should You Use?

The following format is useful for planning either a governmental grant or a private one. It has two basic components:

- Personnel cost
- Non-personnel costs

An optional third component is "Indirect Costs" which pertains to some, but not all, grant applications.

Another element, the "Budget Summary," is written after the completed budget appears at the beginning of the budget section (think back to the proposal summary).

Divide your costs into two columns: "requested" and "donated." The "requested" column represents items that you are asking the funding source to cover; the "donated" column represents items that have either been covered by another source, or were actually donated or contributed to the program. In a federal grant proposal, these sections are known as the "federal share" and the "nonfederal share."

It might help to look at each of these components separately. Funding sources call this process a "budget detail." Each section of the budget is broken down and your budget calculations are shown. If a foundation provides you with forms, the following information will fit into the appropriate spaces.

I. Personnel

A. Salaries & Wages

Enter the information this way:

- Enter the number of employees at the same salary and the same job
- Enter that position title
- Enter the full monthly salary attached to that position, whether full-time or part-time

NOTE: pro-rating salaries for part-time works can be confusing; clarify this information by entering the percentage of time that this person will be working in the program; followed by the number of months that this person will be employed over the course of the grant period)
- Multiply to obtain totals and enter these totals in the appropriate columns, depending upon whether the funds are being requested

of this funding source or coming from another
(Indicate personnel funded by another source with an asterisk (*)
and note the source as additional personnel

If you're not sure how much to budget for individual salaries, make use of a great resource—the Nonprofit Times' Salary Survey (www.nptimes. com). It lists average salaries for nonprofit positions, according to region.

Salaries & Wages	Total	Requested	Donated
Program Director $7,700/mo. @ 100% x 12 mos.	$ 92,400.00	$ 70,000.00	$ 12,400.00
Project Director $4,700/mo. @100% x 12 mos.	$ 56,400.00	$ 56,400.00	
(2) Teachers $3,000/mo./ea. @ 100% x 11 mos.	$ 72,000.00	$ 72,000.00	
Teacher $3,000/mo. @ 50% x 11 mos.	$ 18,000.00	$ 18,000.00	
Administrative Aide $2,400/mo. @ 100% x 12 mos.	$ 28,800.00	$ 14,400.00	$ 14,400.00
Salaries & Wages Total:	$267,600.00	$203,800.00	$26,800.00

We advise you to have salary ranges for as many positions in your organization as possible. If you have them, you may make a note to this section (Example: "All salaries within this budget item represent the second step of the salary range for the position"). You should also attach a copy of your salary schedule to the budget. This procedure prevents you from getting locked into a specific salary. This does, however, depend on your personnel policies. But by using a mid-point salary range for the budget, you allow for the averaging out of salaries for new staff, knowing that some might come in at the first step while others start at the top step. If a funding source advises another way of presenting salaries then follow instructions.

When jobs are created that do not currently exist in your organization, research the appropriate salaries. Look for local organizations that are similar in size and focus then try to identify positions in those organizations that are similar to the new jobs in yours. Use those salaries as a guide. Save the information that you gather, in case the funding source asks how you came up with the salary of the new position. In the salaries and wages section, enter only those positions where money will actually be paid, whether from the proposed grant, from your regular budget, or by some other source. Unpaid volunteers will be entered in the "Consultants and Contract Services" category. The standard and accepted pay rate equivalent for non-professional volunteers is $20.25 per hour.iv

B. Fringe Benefits

Fringe benefits include items like FICA, health insurance, vacation and sick leave, etc. and should be itemized as a separate category in your budget. Don't combine these things with staff salaries. Spell out all of the benefits that will be covered by the grant in detail. Donated benefits can be entered as payroll percentages. Here is an example:

Fringe Benefits	Total	Requested	Donated
State Unemployment Insurance 1%* x $320,800	$ 3,208.00	$ 3,208.00	
Workers' Comp. Policy 3%* x $320,800	$9,624.00	$9,624.00	
FICA 7.65%* x $320,800	$ 24,541.20	$ 24,541.20	
Health Insurance 3 single employees @ $175/mo.* 2 employees w/ dependents @ $385/mo.* (employer pays 100%)	$ 12,950.00	$ 12,950.00	
Extended Disability 5 employees @ $35/mo.*x12 mo.	$ 2,132.00	$ 2,132.00	
Vacation and sick leave 20 wks. @ avg. salary of $1,233/wk.	$ 24,660.00	$ 24,660.00	
Donated fringe benefits for Exec. Dir. based on org. total fringe benefit percentage (26%) of salary ($12,400)	$ 2,604.00		$ 2,604.00
Donated fringe benefits for Project Dir. based on total fringe benefit percentage (26%) of salary ($14,400)	$ 3,744.00		$ 3,744.00
Fringe Benefits Total:	$ 83,463.20	$ 77,115.20	$ 6,348.00

* These rates are meant as examples only. Research local rates when preparing the budget for your individual organization.

There are three kinds of fringe benefits that apply:

Mandated benefits: those required by the state in which you are located. Examples of required benefits are Workers' Compensation Insurance and State Unemployment Insurance (SUI).

Social Security (FICA): Public and private nonprofits are exempt from this but most organizations voluntarily participate.

Voluntary benefits: These vary from organization to organization, and include medical, dental, disability and life insurance, private retirement programs, reimbursement for work-related educational expenses, reimbursement for parking, sabbatical leave, etc. All organizations have some provisions for vacation and sick leave, but rarely think to write them into their budgets. Smaller organizations omit this item from and end up with a financial obligation at the end of the grant period if staff members have not used their vacation time yet. Then they must find the funds to compensate staff for this earned vacation. Avoid this situation by including a figure for vacation and sick leave, if the funding source allows it.

C. Consultant and Contract Services

Paid and unpaid (volunteer) consultants are also listed in a separate section of your budget. You might choose to pay a monthly fee for a bookkeeping service instead of hiring a bookkeeper as part of your staff. The fee must be figured into this section of the budget. The same is true of audit services, evaluation services, and other paid consultant time. If services are volunteered, that must be accounted for here as well. Volunteer time may be allowed by some government funding sources if they require some portion of the grant to be matching funds, or "in kind" contributions developed by the applicant. This raises a question: How do you place a value on the time that someone volunteers? Federal organizations produce varied, even whimsical schedules for evaluating volunteer hours. For example, physicians – $175.00/hr; attorneys – $150.00/hr; teachers – $23.00/hr; social workers – $17.00/hr. Use caution when applying these actual numbers. They are often unrealistic and untrustworthy. Instead, get written statements from the volunteers listing their normal salaries or consultant fees, and their commitment to volunteer like services to your program. It's important to remember, these must be like services. For an accountant to be valued at $75.00/hr. in your program, he/she must be providing accounting services to you, not driving children to and from school. These letters not only establish the value of the volunteered time, but also reveal credibility (these people see your program as so valuable that they are willing to sacrifice time for you).

Consultant & Contract Svcs. Reading Specialist	Total	Requested	Donated
Alice Jones – 4 hrs./wk. @ $85/hr. x 52 wks.	$ 17,680.00	$ 8,840.00	$ 8,840.00
Evaluation Consultant Dr. Patty Smith, Right Start Evaluation Center. – 10 hrs/mo. @ $75/hr. x 12 mos.	$ 9,000.0		$ 9,000.00
Bookkeeping services Balancing Act Bookkeeping – $600/mo. x 12 mos.	$ 7,200.00	$ 7,200.00	
(4) Volunteer tutors 5 hrs./wk. ea. @ $10/hr. x 48 wks.	$ 9,600.00		$ 9,600.00
Consultant & Contract Services Total:	$43,480.00	$16,040.00	$27,440.00

I. Non-Personnel

A. Space Costs

The number one non-personnel item is space costs. This includes rent, space used outside of your office (such as a room at a local school or community center), utilities, maintenance, janitorial services, and renovations. As with all other items in your budget, you must be aware of cost "comparability." If you propose an amount for rent that is much higher than the going rate in your community, be prepared to explain your reasons to the funding source.

Space Costs Office Rental $1,400/mo.	Total	Requested	Donated
	$ 16,800.00	$ 16,800.00	
Tutoring Space contributed by local private school – $150/wk. x 48 wks.	$7,200.00		$7,200.00
Office Janitorial $150/mo. x 12 mos.	$ 1,800.00	$ 1,800.00	
Office Utilities $225/mo. x 12 mo.	$ 2,700.00	$ 2,700.00	
Space Costs Total:	$ 28,500.00	$ 21,300.00	$ 7,200.00

B. Renting and Leasing Equipment

Second in your non-personnel budget is for the rental, lease, or purchase of equipment. This includes things like computers and related equipment, chairs, desks, file cabinets, fax machine, copy equipment, etc. Any unused equipment that your organization currently owns can be applied to this project. It's best to attach an equivalent rental value to these items. For example, rather than buying a new desk for a new staff member, you choose to use one that you already have on hand. Find out what it would cost to rent the desk for a year and put that value into your budget as a contribution from your organization. List items in a table like those you have read in previous sections.

Rental of Equipment	Total	Requested	Donated
(1) Secretarial desk $180.00	$180 ea.	$180.00	

Rental of Equipment	Total	Requested	Donated
(1) Secretarial chair $ 80.00 ea.	$80.00	$ 80.00	
(2) Desks $130 ea.	$260.00	$260.00	
(2) Chairs $80 ea.	$ 160.00	$ 160.00	

(2) Desks donated by applicant rental value of $12/ea./mo. x 12 mos.	$ 288.00		$ 288.00
(4) File cabinets $75 ea.	$ 300.00	$ 300.00	
(2) Computers $500 ea.	$1,000.00	$1,000.00	
(1) Framed scenic wall poster donated	$ 25.00		$ 25.00
(1) Dynamite copier leased @ $85/mo. x 12 mos.	$1,020.00	$1,020.00	
Equipment Total:	$3,313.00	$3,000.00	$313.00

C. Consumable Supplies

Typically, you will use three categories of consumable supplies. All must be listed in your budget. Categories include:

1. Desktop supplies. This would include the usual pens, pencils, stationery, paper clips, staplers, etc. A reasonable cost for these items is $175 to $200 per year per person in your office. Experience will show you whether or not your numbers are sufficient.

2. Copying supplies. Paper and toner are expensive items so list them separately unless you are asked to do otherwise.

3. Program-related consumables. These will depend on your project. An after school program would list things like arts and crafts supplies. A performing arts program would account for stage makeup, costumes, set-building supplies, etc.

Consumable Supplies	Total	Requested	Donated
Desk top supplies 6.5 staff @ $175.00/ea/yr.	$1,137.50	$1,137.50	
Copy Paper 100 reams @ $2.75 ea.	$275.00	$275.00	

Toner for copier 5 @ $85 ea.	$425.00	$425.00
Consumable Supplies Total:	$1,837.50	$1,837.50

D. Travel

You will need to be specific when it comes to travel expenses that you wish to include in the grant budget (mileage, for example). To account for local mileage, project the number of miles you expect each person to accumulate in work-related miles each month. Multiply this by the accepted rate in your geographic area then multiply again by the number of months in the grant period. Out-of-town travel is tricky because you must have an idea of the travel that will be required during the grant. This may be easy for program-related travel (e.g. visiting remote program sites), but is more difficult for things like training and conferences that can come up unexpectedly. These items in your budget should be supported by a statement in your program narrative describing the need for and benefits of all budgeted travel. You might include fees for training, as well as per diem and air travel expenses, in this category.

Be sure to research rates in your area, taking into account things like cost of gasoline.

E. Telephone, Fax, Internet

If you need to install new telephone lines, whether for telephone or fax, get an estimate from the phone company (or appropriate vendor) on the cost of installation. Estimate the average monthly cost per instrument times the number of instruments times the number of months of the project. If you don't have high speed internet access, we recommend that you sign up for a service. In fact, some grantors want to fund high speed internet access as a project cost because it provides so many benefits to your organization. You don't want to appear outdated by using dial-up. Talk to your local service provider for set-up and monthly cost estimates. These costs will also be accounted for in your budget and charted like the others.

F. Other Costs

This category includes items that don't fit neatly into any of your other categories.

Examples include:
- Postage
- Fire, theft, and liability insurance
- Membership dues for professional associations
- Subscriptions to professional periodicals (newsletters, journals, etc.)
- Publications costs

Other Costs	Total	Requested	Donated
Postage	$ 600.00	$ 600.00	
Insurance (Fire, Theft and Liability)	$ 750.00	$ 750.00	
Other Costs Total	$1,350.00	$1,350.00	

II. Indirect Costs

Organizations that operate several different funded projects at once face a unique challenge. The cost to the organization of housing a project may drain the resources of the organization as a whole. Listing indirect costs is an attempt to compensate the organization for these costs and to provide a basis for the sharing of the costs of running a large institution along with the various programs and projects within the organization. The following is a good definition of indirect costs:

Indirect costs are those costs that an organization does not readily identify with a particular project or activity but nevertheless are necessary to the organization's general operation and conduct of activities. The costs of operating and maintaining buildings, grounds and equipment, depreciation, general and departmental administrative salaries and expenses and library costs fall under the category of indirect costs.

In theory, all such costs could be charged directly; practical difficulties, however, make this difficult. Therefore, they are usually grouped into common pool(s) and distributed to those institutional activities that benefit. The end product of this allocation process is an indirect cost rate(s), which is then applied to individual grant and contract awards to determine the amount of indirect costs.

Not every funding source will cover indirect costs. Generally, sources that support higher education will provide them. Some funding sources place a limit on the amount of indirect costs allowed in a given grant situation. Be sure to find out the specifics on what each funding source will allow for indirect costs and plan your budget accordingly.

Budget Summary:

This is what a completed budget might look like:

Project in Entirety	Total	Total Requested	Total Donated
I. Personnel			
A. Salaries and Wages			
B. Fringe Benefits	$267,600.00	$230,800.00	$26,800.00
C. Consultant and	$59,396.20	$ 50,048.20	$ 6,348.00
Contract Services	$43,480.00	$ 16,404.00	$27,440.00
Personnel Total:	$367,476.20	$296,888.00	$60,588.00
II. Non-Personnel			
A. Space Costs			
B. Rental, Lease or	$ 25,500.00	$ 18,300.00	$ 7,200.00
Purchase of Equipment			
C. Consumable Supplies		$ 3,000.00	$ 313.00
D. Travel	$ 3,313.00	$ 1,837.00	
E. Telephone			
F. Other Costs	$ 1,837.50	$ 2,774.00	
	$ 2,540.00	$ 1,350.00	
	$ 1,350.00		
Non-personnel Total:	$37,314.50	$ 29,801.50	$ 7,513.00
Project Total:	**$ 404,790.70**	**$ 326,689.70**	**$ 68,101.00**

III. Establishing Your Need

The problem statement, or needs assessment, is the most important part of your proposal. It reveals your reason for requesting funds.

What's the difference between a needs statement and a problem statement?

- A needs assessment focuses on your client's circumstances, how they need to change, and what you plan to do for them.

- A problem statement looks at that same situation, relates it to similar situations that exist in other communities, and shows why your program can help solve it. The emphasis is on the broader scope of the problem rather individual circumstances.

Whichever focus you choose (you may choose to incorporate both), this section requires some basic elements:

Your statement should be:

1. Clearly related to your goals and purposes

2. Supported by evidence taken from personal examples, statistics, quotes, testimonies, and research

3. Realistic—meaning something that you can do something about over the course of a grant period

4. Relate to problems faced by those you serve, not the needs of your organization

> *"Nothing will work unless you do."*
> *–Maya Angelou*

Needs Assessments and Problem Statements

Proposals that focus on needs usually describe those of a particular group of people or organizations at a specific time in a particular place. While this is a totally legitimate approach, it does limit your funding options to those who either are concerned with those needs in that place, care about the community in general, or appreciate your organization specifically.

Another approach is to present a problem that is found in other places, and your program as potentially valuable to people beyond the limits of your community. This widens your potential for funding by pointing out a greater social benefit. However, it requires more research on your part, more thorough proposal development, and is not always possible to prove.

Here is an example:

The Organization for a Better World has studied autism in children. After studying many groups of autistic children, they have seen improvements in those who followed a strict wheat, gluten, and dairy-free diet. These children show less aggression, more responsiveness, and in some cases appear almost "normal."

The organization has worked with these children and their families for several years with incredible results. Frustrated families have found hope. Doctors, however, are harder to convince. The Organization for a Better World has developed a training program for doctors, educators and other experts who previously struggled to accept the connection between diet and improvements in autism. So far, their program has existed in one specific area. They would like to expand their services and education to include on-line sources, workshops, and other tools. In order to form a convincing case the organization must do several things.

Autistic Children:

Needs Approach vs. Problem Approach

Needs Approach: In order to build a case for need, the organization would provide some background on the problem of autism, but focus on the affected children and families in their Community. Records would be gathered (to satisfy the need for documentation) on the commonness of autism and those who have improved through the proposed program. Include information on waiting list, referrals, and the problems that accompany autism. Since the organization has a well-documented track record, the issue is the extension of its services through education. The objectives in the proposal would be to see more children helped which would lead to improved school performance and reduced emotional stress on families. Grant support might come from those funding medical research and education, those who see the mental health benefits of new approaches for children with autism, foundations that have an interest in the community as a whole, and those who have heard of the organization's reputation.

Problem Approach: A problem statement would look more closely at autism as a disability that extends beyond the bounds of the community. The program would be evaluated based on their potential for helping children in other areas. They might expect to be asked (and consider when writing the proposal):

- Are there other successful programs like yours, in other areas?
- Have others who are not part of your organization, expressed concern for the issue that you are addressing through your program?
- Besides your own clients, who will benefit from what you have observed, learned, or have to offer?
- Are you equipped to move in this broader direction?

After answering the above questions and examining their program, a problem approach would probably be the best choice for The Organization for a Better World.

Expressing Your Need

Whether you go with a problem statement or a need statement, it's best to avoid saying that the problem is a lack of your method or program. For example:

"The **problem** in this community is that we lack services for the disabled."
"Our county **needs** a more accessible senior center."

This approach is rather common and only leads "circular" proposals:

1. The need is a senior center; the problem is a lack of services for the disabled
2. The objective is to create the missing center/services
3. The method? Build the needed facility.

Notice that the senior citizens/individuals with disabilities are not mentioned. Does the community in question have a large population of the group they wish to serve? How does an evaluator know that this new service will meet the needs represented in the community? You need a proven method before you can say, "the need is (fill in what you hope to fund)."

Example 1

Unfortunately, Nevada is not immune to the issue of recidivism. Nevada ranked ninth in the nation in incarcerations per capita and further states that Nevada's prison population has doubled in the last decade. This being the case, it shouldn't come as a surprise that recidivism is prominent in Nevada. In fact, the Nevada Study Committee on Corrections listed it among the state's chief issues in their most recent report to the Governor. In this report, the Committee states: "In an average year, more than 1,600 inmates, or 39 percent of released offenders, expire their sentences and leave prison with no community supervision. More than 20 percent of Nevada's offenders left prison [in 2001] having earned or saved no money and had to be given 'gate money' to get home. Thus, it is not surprising that 26 percent of NDOC's annual intake consists of parole violators returning to custody."

Recognizing this issue, and in response to the Committee's request, the State provided over $2 million to build Casa Grande, a state-run transitional housing project in Las Vegas for inmates at the end of their sentences. Casa Grande opened in December 2005 with a capacity of 400 men and has proven successful thus far. However, the building of this facility leaves a huge gap in transitional services for Northern Nevada inmates as no such state-funded services currently exist outside of Southern Nevada.

The Northern Nevada Center for Restitution, located in downtown Reno, offers services similar to Casa Grande; however, their capacity is just 95 men. With NDOC reporting that over 5,000 Nevada inmates are released each year, there is still a great need for services to help former local offenders reintegrate into society. Based on the above evidence, it is absolutely vital that appropriate transitional programming be offered to released offenders in Northern Nevada. Without such, the prison system, the families of inmates and the residents of Northern Nevada as a whole will continue to be affected by recidivism in our local communities.

Example 2

There are over two million children in the U.S. today who have one or both parents in prison, (Federal Resource Center for the Children of Prisoners). The majority of these children are under ten years old. Losing a parent to prison can affect every aspect of a child's life. Additionally, weakened ties to the incarcerated parent are linked to poor school performance, increased delinquency, disruption in their psychological development and maturational process and increased risk of intergenerational incarceration. Tragically, children of offenders are six times more likely than their peers to end up in prison. In fact, if intervention measures aren't taken, 70% of these children, or 1.4 million young people, will have at least one encounter with the criminal justice system (U.S. Senate Report 106-404).

Conversely, contact that helps to maintain the family bond during incarceration benefits both the parent and the child, reducing the strain of separation, increasing the odds of successful reunification and, even more importantly, decreasing the likelihood of the children being incarcerated themselves or developing severe emotional difficulties later in their lives. Unfortunately, the many barriers to this contact often result in no contact at all. We all suffer in this tragedy: parents, children, and the community that pays in increased taxes for social services and the justice system.

Through Angel Tree, a project of Prison Fellowship Ministries and Project BLESS, prisoners are able to touch the lives of their children at Christmas, the toughest of times for both the parent and the child. Prisoners can sign up to have volunteers deliver gifts and a personal message to their children from the absent parent. This provides these children with reassurance that they are neither forgotten nor unloved.

In both of these problem/need statements, real people are the focus rather than a generic "problem" that can only be met by the organization.

Exercise:

Answer the questions using the examples above.
When evaluating your problem/need statement, a reviewer will want to know:

1. What organization or group of people are you most concerned with?

_____

_____

_____

2. What problem or need does your organization focus on?

_____

_____

_____

3. Is this a problem that can change for the better over a grant period?

_____

_____

_____

4. What direction is your need statement moving in?

_____

_____

_____

5. Is your statement concerned with the clients' needs or your organization's needs?

_____

_____

_____

Why it's so important to understand the problem

A mental health facility is having great success in treating patients within their residential treatment center. Over the past seven years it has tracked the progress of its former patients, finding that those who maintained employment with higher potential for advancement and salary remained stabilized for longer periods of time than those who were unemployed or had low paying/low advancement jobs.

Shortly after gathering this research, they discovered that several large companies had their headquarters within sixty miles of the facility. Two of these companies had training programs. In addition to this, several former patients had applied with these companies, only to be turned down. Knowing that training and jobs were open at both companies and that many current patients showed interest in the opportunities, the staff came up with an idea.

The mental health center created a proposal for vocational training programs to be offered by these companies at the facility. The training program would have its own large building, complete with classrooms, computers, and appropriate equipment. They spent months planning the details and were very excited. But they failed to consider one important detail:

They assumed that the patients receiving this training would have an open door to employment with these companies. But, they had no reason to expect such a thing. They also assumed that the rejections of employment had been connected to lack of training. What if, the former patients had actually been rejected because of their backgrounds of mental instability? They could go through a rigorous training program and still be turned down for employment. In this case, a proposal to cover professional training for specific companies would be a waste of money and time.

A better approach would be for representatives from the facility to convince these same companies to consider hiring a few qualified patients on a trial basis (after they left the hospital). It would eliminate the need for an expensive training program and possibly open up opportunities for future patients, if the trial worked out.

This organization was prepared to jump head first into a training program because it saw potential for its patients. It assumed that if its graduates had some background appropriate to the jobs, or trainee positions, they would be hired more frequently. In reality, past applicants from the facility were repeatedly turned down for both employment and training at these two companies. Why? Lack of skill? Employer prejudice? Completely unrelated reasons? If a lack of skills were the reason for applicants being turned down, then perhaps skills training would make sense. If, on the other hand, pre-conceived notions about mental illness were the issue, then skills training were not the answer. A project focused on community education and changing attitudes might help more.

Too often applicants leap quickly into innovative programs or activities without considering all the facts. In order to create a program that accomplishes objectives, as opposed to just conducts activities, an organization must do a thorough examination.

Here is an approach to a problem statement:

Problem Statement/Needs Assessment:

The Effects of Recidivism

Recidivism is a growing epidemic in America. Defined as the tendency to relapse into a previous undesirable type of behavior, especially crime, the Federal Bureau of Justice Statistics reports a steady increase in the national recidivism rate over the past 20 years. The Bureau's most recent study states that 67.5 percent of released prisoners were rearrested for a new crime within three years of their release. According to the same study, nearly two-thirds of all recidivism occurred within the first year.

The effects of recidivism stretch well beyond the individual offender. Each year, millions of tax dollars are poured into state and federal prisons as a result of former offenders returning to prison. Locally, the Nevada Department of Corrections (NDOC) reports that it costs approximately $44.28 per inmate per day they are in prison. In 2004, the average cost per year per inmate was over $17,600 in Nevada. With an estimated 1,400 inmates returning to Nevada prisons on new charges after their release each year, every Nevada taxpayer feels the effects of recidivism.

Even deeper are the effects recidivism has on the offender's family. When the offender is the sole breadwinner for his family, often the family is forced onto welfare. For children, losing a parent to prison affects multiple aspects of their lives, from financial hardships to changed living circumstances and a myriad of emotional issues. With their parent in prison, ties between the parent and child are weakened. These weakened ties are linked to poor school performance, increased delinquency, and disruption in their psychological development and maturational process. In a 2002 report to Governor Kenny Guinn, The Nevada Study Committee on Corrections reported that children of inmates are five times more likely than their peers to end up in prison.

Recidivism Causes & Prevention

While many factors can lead a former offender back to a life of crime, certain characteristics are consistent across the board. The Texas Department of Criminal Justice lists the following among the leading causes of recidivism:

1. Literacy. Criminal activity and a lack of education are inextricably linked. The Federal Bureau of Justice Statistics (BJS) reports that just 21 percent of inmates graduated from high school, and an additional 29 percent hold a GED. Nearly 40 percent did not complete a high school education, and 14 percent of those have an eighth grade education or less. If offenders aren't given the opportunity to expand their education and develop job skills, they are much more likely to return to a life of crime upon their release.

2. Employment. Obtaining employment is one of the most important factors for preventing a return to prison, but it is also one of the most difficult tasks for a recently released offender. Given the overall low educational attainment by former inmates, employment can be difficult to find. These challenges are often compounded by the fact that many employers are reluctant to hire an individual with a criminal record, and even further complicated given many recently released offenders don't have basic personal documentation required for employment, such as a driver's license or birth certificate. Discouraged by a lack of options to earn an honest wage, many offenders return to life of crime.

A sub-issue stemming from a lack of employment is a lack of a viable place to live. Without a source of income, former offenders are unable to pay rent and are often forced to live either on the streets or with family or friends. In a recent article, the Vera Institute for Justice reported, "Many people preparing to leave prisons and jails do not have a home. They often return to communities where persistent poverty and lack of jobs and affordable housing make finding a permanent home difficult." Unfortunately, former offenders often end up in the same neighborhoods with the same cohorts that led them to a life of crime in the first place. Without a stable place to live and positive reinforcement from those around them, an offender's likelihood of re-arrest skyrockets.

New Horizon Program Overview

The New Horizon Center helps fill this vital need in our community. Our transitional home in Lemmon Valley can house up to eight men, and our wrap-around services and personal, individualized care creates the ideal environment for successful reintegration.

The proposal then goes on to explain how the program works, followed by their current objectives. It is easy to read, skips all the jargon, and clearly expresses the need that they strive to meet.

Problem Statement Documentation

It is vital that you distinguish between a national problem and one that exists in your community. Take homelessness for example. Showing it as a national problem would require statistics and expert testimony, obtained through federal organizations. Published records of congressional hearings are another valuable and underused source (be sure to keep copies to legitimize your research).

National statistics may not necessarily apply to your community. They could, be valuable for comparative statistics, however. How does the homeless population in your area compare with the national or state average?

Next, you want to gather statistics for your state and community.

Issues related to educational, health and other problems vary widely from community to community. You must present evidence that a problem truly exists in the community served by your organization. Rather than saying, "based on national statistics, we estimate that homelessness in Retched County is . . ." For this, you need to locate local sources. If you can't find statistics, you might try taking a local survey (hint: there are websites that allow you to create them for free—SurveyMonkey.com for example). But there is also a simpler way.

Case in Point:

Your organization is concerned with the rising pregnancy rate among local teen girls. In your research, you haven't found any recorded local statistics on the problem. You can begin your documentation by identifying agencies and individuals who would know about this problem in the school and surrounding area. Write a brief letter, explaining who you are, why you are concerned, and how you plan to help. One option might be to invite the recipient to a meeting set for the near future. Your attached questionnaire could include the following:

1. What are your thoughts regarding this problem or need?
2. What evidence can you provide to support the existence of this problem?
3. Do you know of any other local organizations concerned with the situation? What kind of action are they currently taking?

Limit questions to a few. That should give you enough to gather information, plan meetings, and discuss the problem further. At the same time, valuable relationships can be formed through these contacts.

Details, Details
Does your problem statement/needs assessment:

- Relate to your organization's purposes and goals
- Have reasonable dimensions
- Include statistics and other concrete evidence
- Include statements from authorities
- Relate to the needs of your clients or those who will benefit
- Include input from clients or affected individuals
- Avoid assumptions
- Use clear, jargon-free language
- Get to the point
- Keep your interest

III. Objectives

As you plan your program or project designed to solve a problem or meet a need, you need to establish objectives you plan to reach. In your planning you probably thought something such as, "If we do this, we'll get this result." Those are your objectives.

Program objectives are "outcomes" of your activities. Be careful not to confuse them with the activities themselves, or the methods. Activities or methods are the means; objectives or outcomes are the ends. Too often, grant seekers confuse the two. Distinguishing between them is of critical importance in planning programs and writing proposals. Objectives are problem-related outcomes of your program.

How do you know if you are starting in the right place? Words like those listed below indicate a method rather than an objective:

We strive to provide . . .

to create...

to offer...

to reach out to...

The words below refer to an objective:

Our goal is to increase...

to decrease...

to eliminate...

Think of your program objective(s) as the measuring stick for judging the effectiveness of your program. So your objective should:

Tell who
is going to be doing:
What...
When...
How much...
How you will measure
success/progress..

"It takes a lot of courage to show your dreams to someone else."
–Erma Bombeck

Communicating Your Objective

Let's say that we want to come up with a measurable objective for this grant-writing workshop. In order to do this we give tests to participants on terminology, program evaluation, measurable objectives, etc. At the end of the workshop, we test you again. We might express our objective something like this:

> At the end of the 3-day workshop, all participants will show some improvement in knowledge of test topics. At least 75% of participants will improve their score by 90%.

The above objective tells the evaluator that we are dedicated to communicating certain information to a group in a way that allows them to learn and absorb the material. This material will be taught over a specific period of time (3 days) with a planned method for evaluating improvement (a pre-test and a post-test). Notice that the objective does not mention using the results for anything other than measuring success of each individual workshop. Anything more would require another objective. For example, if we wanted to measure the success of our workshop over time we might say:

> By the end of the first year, 25 to 50% of participants, each representing different non-profits and programs, will write and submit proposals that find funding. Another 30% will write two or more successful grants.

These objectives are specific and measurable. The success of the program is determined by whether or not the objective is met.

Since objectives and problem statements are so closely related let's examine them separately.

Problem Statement/Needs Assessment:

> In a school district of 52,609 students, grades K-12, 14.7% of families are below poverty level. As a result, their children and teens suffer from lack of adequate nutrition, due to the limited income from which they can purchase food. Although the reasons behind nutrition-related problems are complex, inadequate income is a major contributor. Other factors include lack of education, complications of disease, sedentary lifestyles, mental and emotional illnesses, isolation, lack of suitable preparation and storage facilities (such as refrigerators and stoves), consumer confusion and misinformation,

and the overabundance of foods with little or no nutritional value. High cost of nutritious food like milk, eggs, and fresh produce also plays a role.

Adequate food and nutrition are essential to learning. Studies show that students who eat breakfast, for example, perform better on tests. Good nutrition is one of the keys to quality of life and quality of education. Children who eat well are better equipped to concentrate on, absorb, and retain material. A student who arrives at school on an empty stomach, or with food that is low in vitamins and nutrition, is already behind.

Objectives:
The objective of this program is to improve opportunities for low-income families (particularly those with school-aged, middle school and high school students at home) to gain access to federal and community food programs, as well as education in shopping for and preparing wholesome foods that they can afford.

The objective of "improving opportunities" is not measurable. There is also no clear indicator that more families will participate in these food programs or take advantage of the education offered. The "objective" above is really a "method." All that follows the "by . . ." is method. In order to follow the problem with a clear objective, we need to see evidence that the programs target population will show improvement in diet, overall health, and especially school performance.

Clearly, this applicant has not examined the problem in detail. Rather, the applicant has a program in mind, along with some proposed program activities. Obviously, the "lack of education" (who lacks knowledge about what?) will call for an educational component; "lack of suitable preparation and storage" is setting us up for a program providing such things. Still, the problem statement and objective are lacking. They raise questions regarding the potential benefit of a program.

Here's a proposal with a well-stated problem and objective:

Excerpt from Problem Statement/Needs Assessment:

Forced into Homelessness

> Roughly, 1% of Americans become homeless each year. For the majority of these individuals, homelessness is a temporary circumstance brought on by social and economic factors beyond their control. Common reasons for homelessness include unemployment,

extremely low paying jobs, poor economy, and lack of affordable housing, prolonged health problems, and **mental illness.**

When asked to identify their greatest needs, or the one thing that kept them homeless, people named the following:
- 42% - Finding a job
- 38% - Finding affordable housing

In spite of their efforts, shelters are unable to meet the constant and growing need. In 2008, 37% of requests for emergency housing went unmet due to lack of resources. For a family with no home the picture was even bleaker as 52% of their requests were denied. The situation is even sadder in rural areas, where the level of homelessness is high but shelters are rare.

Homelessness in Hope County

Hope County is a community that relies on tourism, as well as seasonal industries like fishing and lumber, for its survival. Our area is small, yet we support a high population of homeless individuals. In the warmer months, we can see up to 2,500 homeless people. An unfortunately high percentage of this number includes children and teens whose parents have become unemployed or suffered an unusually slow year (often due to weather or other unforeseeable problems). Though we have a shelter, our waiting list is long. County Services lists emergency shelter and related support services as Hope County's number one need. Congressman Joe Miller, of the 54th District, stressed the issue of homelessness in a recent address, pushing for support of our organization's proposed programs (a letter of endorsement is attached).

Temporary shelters relieve the immediate crisis of those who are willing and eager to improve their circumstances. It is critical that such individuals and families find safe shelter that also offers services like job counseling, assistance in finding affordable housing, referrals to available programs, and opportunity for consistent physical and mental healthcare as they transition back into self-sufficiency.

Community organizations that provide such services have proven successful again and again. There is, however, a shortage of programs that offer the variety of services necessary, and none are located in Hope County.

Seeing the Big Picture

Helping the homeless is more than a matter of conscience; it is a matter of economics. Countless tax dollars and volunteer hours are spent supporting shelters and other services to the homeless. In addition to this, homeless men and women have an increased occurrence of:

- *Costly Medical Needs:* Conditions that would normally be easily treated often progress into more serious problems due to poor diet and living situations. The stress and uncertainty of daily survival add to existing physical or mental issues. If hospitalized they often require longer hospital stays due to complications and neglected problems. In fact, they require an average of four days more than non-homeless individuals who are hospitalized for the same physical conditions, and up to 100 days longer for mental issues.

- *Incarceration:* Homeless adults tend to spend more time in jail. Crimes usually involve loitering or pan handling. According to a University of Texas survey, each homeless individual costs taxpayers $14,480 per year in law enforcement alone.

- *Lengthy Stays in Emergency Shelters:* Emergency shelters often become long-term "homes" for those with no other option. The cost of a bed through HUD's Emergency Shelter Grants program is approximately $8,067. Ironically, this is more than the average annual cost of a federal housing subsidy.

- *Loss of Productivity:* If homelessness leads to prison time or health problems, productivity drops, along with prospects for future success. Consequently, they have even more obstacles to overcome in becoming a contributing member of society. Homeless children face gaps in their education that lower their chances of future achievement and eventually perpetuate the cycle of poverty.

Objectives:

A Place for Us endeavors to meet the following goals in our first year of operation:

- Provide 300 homeless individuals and families with shelter.

- Enable 85% of those served to participate in an organized self-sufficiency program.

- 60% will successfully complete the self-sufficiency program.

- Of those who participate in the self-sufficiency program, 45% will move into sustainable housing arrangements (the level of independency will depend on capability).

- Fifty percent of those who transfer into housing will continue to utilize the services offered at A Place for Us, but as an "out-client."

One hundred percent will be allowed to access information from time to time. Examples of those who might need continued assistance from us would be the disabled, mentally ill, and veterans. Clients may also need to contact us when there are changes in the social programs they are connected with.

It is projected that 300 people will seek shelter annually, through A Place for Us. Many will stay only a few nights. Those who need to stay longer will be required to meet specific guidelines in order to participate in A Place for Us: Steps to Self-Sufficiency. Seventy-five percent of the shelter's available space will be occupied by participants in the program. All residents, whether in the program or not, along with extremely poor members of Hope County, will have the following daily services available:

- Meals
- Showers
- Laundry
- Telephone and Internet access
- Chaplain services, as well as weekly chapel
- Educational programs

This proposal clearly states their goals in measurable terms. It transitions smoothly from problem to objective. Nicer still, it is interesting and easy to read.

Process Objectives

The objectives cited so far are often referred to as "behavioral" or "performance" objectives. They are also called "program" or "outcome" objectives. Fine lines distinguish one from another but all involve the results of a program.

Process objectives are quite different. These refer to the completion of tasks that you plan to accomplish over the course of the program or grant period.

For example:

"We will recruit and train 50 eligible participants by the end of the first 90 days of the grant period." Process objectives will be covered in more detail in the methodology section. Don't confuse process objective with outcome objective. Successful recruitment does not guarantee that a participant will benefit from your services. They are two separate issues. Outcome objectives relate to the benefits of your program. Goals related to training, education, counseling, or recruitment of X number of people in a given amount of time relate to the process objective.

Promises, Promises:
How much change should your strive for?

A proposal for an in-patient, addiction recovery facility claimed that 92% of its clients were drug and alcohol free. They promised similar results in a program for juvenile addicts. Reviewers were hesitant to believe the numbers. Further examination revealed that the percentage was based on a small population of clients—those who had completed the program. Patients who had dropped out were not included in the statistics. A realistic estimate of benefits should be based on the experience of your organization and a study of the success of similar programs.

Perhaps you find it difficult to speculate on a specific percentage gain. Sometimes such progress is a guessing game. In that case state that you will see a "statistically significant" increase in benefit, meaning that, statistically, your results could not have occurred as a result of coincidence. It is always a good idea to seek the help of someone within your organization (or even outside) who has a background in statistics.

Coming up with benchmarks takes time but it is a necessary part of the process. And yes, you can measure "changed lives" through benchmarks.

Details, Details

In stating your objectives, have you:

- Described the outcome(s) of your program
- Related the outcome to the problem
- Described your objectives instead of your methods
- Defined the population that you are serving
- Listed a specific timeline for when the objectives will be met
- Attached numbers to your objectives

IV. Methods

After you have stated problems and needs, along with your clear objectives, you will need to describe your methods for accomplishing the objectives. Methods, activities, strategies, and procedures can be used interchangeably in your proposal but all refer to how you will reach your desired outcome. As in all other areas of the proposal, the section describing your methods must flow smoothly from objectives section. Your methods should be:

- Clear
- Simple
- Understandable
- Accompanied by an explanation of why you chose them
- Clear on why you think these methods will work

Justifying your methods usually involves incorporating examples of your past methods and successes.

How Long Should the Methods Section be?

There is no need to ramble on about every activity, procedure, and plan. At the same time, you don't want to be so brief that you leave the reviewer doubting whether you have a plan in place at all. State the most important methods that will help you reach your objectives—the most interesting, innovative, or organized.

Here is an example of a methods section that is a bit too short:

Methods:

The State of the Arts summer theater program will involve rehearsing and performing two full-scale musical productions, performed by 50-75 children and youth. Five performances of each will take place at the Masquerade Theater, in addition to additional performances at Cultured County's annual Summer Nights Arts Festival.

"Action and reaction, ebb and flow, trial and error, change – this is the rhythm of living. Out of our over-confidence, fear; out of our fear, clearer vision, fresh hope. And out of hope, progress."
– Bruce Barton

The following example comes from a long and detailed proposal that requires a more lengthy methods section.

Our Method: SkyView Title 1 Program is designed to improve the overall achievement of educationally disadvantaged children. All components of our program, from teacher training to specific services, operate with this result in mind. This request pertains specifically to teacher training. We will use skilled specialists and teachers who have received intense training in recognizing and educating children based on their unique strengths and weakness. The following describes our plan:

Staff Selection

The SkyView Program will employ 20 skills specialists, 15 reading specialists, 10 math specialists and 30 instructional aides, and 5 administrative staff. All specialists must be accredited teachers; instructional aides must have experience working with disadvantaged or special needs students. All staff will be required to possess knowledge of individualized instructional techniques and have the ability to organize workshops, establish classroom activities and stations, and work easily with other teachers, aides and students. The instructional aides must understand the unique structure of individualized instruction and have the ability to prepare classroom materials, with both individual students and small groups, and assist in reading and math instruction. First priority will be given to aides and teachers who have worked in our program before.

Staff Training

To make the program a success, SkyView will first train the skills specialists and aides. After training, they will organize in-service workshops at their respective schools to educate classroom teachers in the program, help them establish learning stations, and illustrate ways of creating supplementary learning materials that correspond with the program's educational objectives.

The intensive training of the skills specialists and aides will occur throughout the 2008-09 school year. Following is the calendar of activities from August 2008 through June 2009:

August 2008:
- Program orientation in-service workshop: principals, skills specialists, and staff
- District Parent Advisory Board meeting
- In-service for SkyView instructional aides conducted by skills specialists and office staff

September 2008:
- General session instructional aides: focus for 2008-09; create a calendar of monthly in-service
- Skills specialists and staff: overview of priorities and program for 2008-09
- Parent Workshop: guidelines, program, and parent involvement for 2008-09
- District Parent Advisory Committee Meeting
- Instructional aides: implementation of the program and instruction on individualized education
- Title 1 skills specialists: facilitating program implementation and research design

(Calendar continues through June 2009.)

In summer 2008, all skills specialists and aides will attend a training that offers four different types of learning situations. Group workshops, which the specialists attend together, cover such topics as scheduling students in learning centers, new methods for teaching basic skills, and teaching writing skills. Each specialist will have a one-on-one session with a curriculum consultant, emphasizing the importance of adapting a classroom management system to a teacher's unique style of teaching and needs. In addition, specialists will teach summer school classes (aides will be encouraged to assist), incorporating the ideas they gather. A major part of the summer training will be the development of "tool kits." The specialists make the materials for their own kits, which will be used in conjunction with the learning stations at their respective schools. The kits contain games, worksheets, and other materials and are color-coded to correspond to program objectives and make filing easier.

The in-service training of skills specialists and aides will continue during the 2008-09 school year. They will visit schools and classrooms, continue in-service training, develop models of instruction, and continue developing and screening new learning materials for Title I students.

The skills specialists will plan in-service training programs for classroom teachers at their respective schools at least once a month.

Who will Participate?

The schools receiving Title I funds in SkyView will be selected according to the percentage of children from families receiving Temporary Assistance for Needy Families (TANF). The participating schools will have 15 to 40 percent of their student population from TANF families; schools with less than 15 percent of TANF cases will not be eligible for Title I services.

Within our 12 participating schools, Title I students will be selected on the basis of standardized test scores. Any student who scores a year or more below grade level is considered educationally disadvantaged. In 2006-07, the enrollment in each participating school and the number of Title I students were as follows below:

School	Total Enrollment	# of eligible Title I students	School	Total Enrollment	# of eligible Title I students
#1	343	150	#6	122	35
#2	492	170	#7	323	110
#3	326	210	#8	475	190
#4	522	266	#9	859	326
#5	588	170	#10	269	50

Classroom teachers, assisted by both district and Title I skills specialists, will test and place all students on a reading and math skills continuum, using existing criterion reference tests. In Title I schools, there will be a skills specialist (either district or Title I salaried) for each grade level; other schools may have one skills specialist for every two or three grades, depending on a school's size. The skills specialists will divide their time among all teachers at their grade level; beginning in 2008-09 each skills specialist will be assigned to one classroom teacher for most of the day. However, they will also work with the other teachers in the creation of learning centers and the development of new materials.

The skills specialists, both district and Title I, will concentrate their attention on the lowest achieving students in each classroom.

Our Rationale

An individualized learning structure has the advantage over more traditional programs in that lessons are tailored to each student's fundamental needs. Individualized instruction takes the student at the level of his accomplishment and builds on already known skills to learn new skills. SkyView's efforts over the past five years have demonstrated the potential of this program. Of 40 students who participated in a pilot program last year, 307, or 75 percent, advanced by more than two grade levels over a period of nine months.

This methods section is quite meticulous. It also addresses key elements that should be included in most methods sections.

Here is an example from another arts program. Notice that it paints a much clearer picture than the first without droning on.

Methods:

The Rising Stars theater program will be open to students aged 10-18. The Glacier Point School district has 18 schools. Home schooled students will also be invited to participate. For this reason, a wide range of ethnic and economic backgrounds will be represented.

Two plays will be presented to schools throughout the district. One of these five months will be used for rehearsal and for final arrangements on booking of the shows. The subject matter of the plays will relate to the literature and history lessons being studied in classrooms. English and history teachers from local schools will serve as an Advisory Committee staff to discuss material with the theater staff. Their recommendations to date are contained in the attached report.

As has been discussed with the teacher/advisors, presentations will focus on high points and important moments in each given story. Students will be involved, not only in the acting, set design, and overall production, but also discussions of the material.

Programs utilizing a theatrical presentation in the schools have been offered to primary and secondary age students in Glacier Point by Lights Up Repertory Company. Performances dealt with prejudice, problems of drug abuse, and other important issues. While no information was sought on the impact of these presentations, 90 percent of the schools requested an additional program or wished the same program to be repeated again. A similar theater program has been presented in England for ten years. Initiated in 2002 to augment normal learning techniques, this program has had remarkable success. A 2004 survey conducted by the Community Committee on Education stated "Students involved in Lights Up and similar performances increased their grades by an average of 10 to 20 percent" compared to students in other classes who did not see the performances. In addition, school attendance increased, both for performance days and also for classes to which the performances were related."

This methods section satisfies all of the requirements, including describing potential benefits.

Time Charts

Earlier you read an outline of training that would take place as part of a Title 1 Educational program. This could have also been listed on a time chart (such as a spreadsheet) or graph. The same is true of the arts program (listing their audition, rehearsal, and performance schedule for example). Time charts make such information readable, concise, and easy to follow.

Event/Date	Jul-08	Aug-08	Sep-08	Oct-08	Nov-08	Dec-08	Jan-09	Feb-09	Mar-09	Apr-09	May-09	Jun-09	Jul-09
1. Recruit new staff	✓												
2. Pre-program training		✓											
3. Meet with referral organizations						✓							
4. Prepare client recruitment materials			✓										
5. Finalize intake criteria		✓											
6. Finalize training curriculum		✓											
7. Recruit initial 50 clients								✓					
8. Finalize client pre-test					✓								
9. Administer pre-test to 50		✓											
10. Conduct first workshop												✓	

Setting up tasks or activities in this fashion can be an aid to program planning. Without such a plan, certain necessary steps might be overlooked.

Details, Details
Does your "methods" section:

- Flow naturally from your problems/needs and objectives
- Clearly describe your program's activities
- State your reasons for selecting activities
- Show the sequence of activities
- Discuss how you will staff the program(s)
- Describe clients and client selection
- Present a reasonable scope of activities that can be accomplished within the time allotted and available resources

V. Planning & Evaluation

In the final "product" of a grant proposal, you will be expected to provide evaluation information as follows. This section is also to be used in your initial planning because planning and evaluation are simply different ways of looking at the program or project; the one occurring before you implement the program or project, the other during and after.

Funding sources will usually require that you have some kind of evaluation process in place and include it in your proposal. The evaluation should have two components:

Component 1:
Program Evaluation (also known as product, impact, or summative evaluation)

A good program evaluation measures:
- The results of your program
- Success in achieving its objectives
- How much of that success can be connected with the program

Component 2:
Process Evaluation

Your process evaluation should:
- Examine the conduct of the program
- Determine whether the program has been conducted as planned
- Examine the connection between individual results and the program

"Always bear in mind that your own resolution to succeed is more important than any other."

–Abraham Lincoln

Why are Evaluations so Important?

There are many reasons.

1. They are usually required
2. Creating your own reduces the chance of a funding source conducting its own evaluation of your program, using methods that you might not be prepared for.
3. It forces you to examine your objectives, methods, and whether or not you can really achieve what you are setting out to do
4. It allows you to make changes early on when you see that your efforts are not having the desired results
5. Evaluations provide data when it comes time to make important decisions
6. Evaluation can provide staff with data to reinforce their efforts or to recommend new directions
7. Policy makers can use evaluation data as a tool in directing the organization into productive channels
8. When evaluations show evidence of the strengths of your programs, they can provide motivation to clients and potential clients
9. Evidence of prior efforts reassures current and future funding sources of your diligence and sincerity
10. Evaluative data is a powerful instrument for public relations
11. Evaluations can help others in your field to anticipate problems in implementing similar programs and provide yardsticks for measuring success.

Who Should Conduct your Evaluation?

Is it best for one of your own staff members to evaluate a program or should your hire someone from "the outside?" Do you need to hire a professional?

Calling on an unbiased outsider who has no vested interest in your program or its success may be the best move. Not only will a professional approach be used when planning and conducting the evaluation, but it can also add to the credibility of your proposal if the funder sees that you are willing to invest in a top notch examination. One drawback, however, is the cost involved in hiring a professional evaluator.

Evaluations that come from within will be performed by one who knows more about the real issues in the program, but may also be jaded by awareness that a poor evaluation could jeopardize the organization's reputation and opportunities for future funding. If you have the freedom to choose one approach over the other, take these points into consideration:

If an outsider performs the evaluation:
- Can your organization afford it financially?
- Will the evaluator agree to forego a fee or a percentage of the fee if the project is not funded?
- Will the evaluator assist in designing the program?
- If the program is already set in stone, is the evaluator willing to do the evaluation only (some won't)?
- Will the evaluator's reputation enhance the credibility of your proposal?
- Do you have reason to believe that the evaluator will try to please you?

If staff performs it:
- What can you pay them?
- Does anyone have experience or knowledge in the area of evaluation?
- Will the evaluation process keep them from performing other required duties?
- Will the evaluation threaten staff or reduce the accuracy of the evaluation?
-

Neither choice is right or wrong. Often your decision will depend on financial resources. Your philosophy will come into play as well. Whichever route you choose, the key issue is the accuracy and validity of information gathered and how it will benefit your program.

"Can't We Just Skip This Part?"

It might be tempting to skip the evaluation section completely. Many proposal writers allow themselves to be scared off by things like . . .

A daunting required process, such as formal weekly meetings or records that require explicit detail, (some of which you don't understand or don't apply to your type of program)

Knowledge that the foundation plans to call in their own expert to "assure success"

The requirements seem ridiculous and endless ("The evaluation consists of the ongoing review of the data derived from the survey and examination obtained at the initial interview so that both client and program needs can be determined.")

Regardless of intimidating lingo and requirements, coming up with your own evaluation process will show funders just how serious you are about making this program a success.

Evaluations made simple

Evaluations aren't as scary as they sound. If your program has a well-defined purpose and clear objectives then you can expect specific questions to be answered in your evaluation. For example, if the purpose of your program were to train unemployed single moms, you would want to answer questions like these:

1. What percentage of the trainees found employment after completing training?

2. How many retained their jobs for at least a year? Two years? Etc.

3. What was the range and average salary of those placed in jobs after training?

4. To what extent did the implemented program resemble the program you originally planned?

5. Which aspects of the program clearly attributed to the success?

Similarly, if the objective of a program is an improvement in the overall health of schoolchildren living at or below poverty level, you will need to gather data to establish any change in health that occurs during and after the program. Gathering information before the program begins is an important reason for making an evaluation plan part of a proposal. If change occurs, you must know where the client is at the beginning of the program so that you have a base of comparison at the end of it.

Creating Your Evaluation, Step By Step

Incorporate these steps when developing the evaluation portion of your proposal:

Step 1 – Make sure your program objectives are clear.
Remember; evaluation requires that your objectives are clear and measurable. If you are using an outside expert for your evaluation, ask him or her to examine the objectives that have been laid out for clarity and measurability. If need be, rewrite them to insure that a product evaluation can be performed.

Step 2 – Consider who will read the evaluation.
People inside your organization may have one set of questions that they want answered while outsiders want to know other things. For example, your organization may be questioned about its services to disabled students. School board members, a local politician, and donor might

feel that your program serves the physically disabled better than it does the developmentally disabled. In this case, you would need to pay close attention to data that describes the diversity of those you serve, as well as examining services and benefits to students with specific types of disabilities. You can base evaluation questions on who will be reading the evaluation.

Step 3 - Will you need a process evaluation, a product evaluation, or both? Often this will depend on the requirements of your funding sources. Be certain that you know exactly what they want. Since every funding source is different, you will want to include both types of evaluation in your proposal.

Step 4 – Decide who will conduct the evaluation.
Will someone within your organization conduct it or will you hire someone? Finances may be the deciding factor. You will also need to find out if the funding source will evaluate the program. Will you be able to utilize the funding source evaluations to your benefit, or will it require more work on your part? Will your program staff participate as evaluators? This may work to your advantage. It could also be incredibly time-consuming or require expertise that nobody on staff has. Bias is another concern. This is a case where a consultant might be a good choice.

Step 5 – Decide if your evaluation needs analysis of cost benefit/or cost-effectiveness. This type of analysis relates the costs of a program with its benefits. So if two similar programs have approximately the same social benefits, the one that costs less would be considered more cost-effective. With increasing concern about the costs of social programs, an analysis of costs vs. benefits would be appropriate, whenever possible. For example, a community alternative to imprisonment for drug offenders was initially denied funding. A rewritten proposal, however, focused on the fact that while the organization's recidivism rate was similar to that of a state institution, the cost per offender was one-fourth what the state institution spent. The project was funded based on this cost comparison.

Step 6 – Determine how evaluation data will be collected. How you collect data will depend on the nature of your program, how the typical evaluation in your field is performed, the degree of rigor you wish to achieve, and your resources. Some methods include pre- and post-testing; interview procedures; observation of and by clients and staff, examining statistics.

Step 7 – Determining how the evaluation data will be analyzed.
If data is to be analyzed based on statistics, the techniques must be considered when planning the evaluation (different statistical techniques require different methods of data collection). A simple questionnaire can be so poorly designed, resulting in a difficult task when it comes

time to transfer the information. Open-ended interviews, to be encoded for purposes of comparison, may require months of analysis merely to establish the criteria for coding. If the appropriate data is not collected in the appropriate way, analysis may be useless, if not impossible.

Step 8 – Determine how the information will be reported.

What does the funding source require? How and when will evaluation information be returned to staff in order to allow for program change and improvement? Should the actual report be prepared in more than one version, for presentation to the several audiences that may be interested? It's important to find out ahead of time so you don't have to scramble later.

Sample Evaluation

A local police department plans to expand its crime prevention program. The objective is to "reduce losses to life and property by reducing the number of crimes in the community." More specifically, the department wishes to reduce the number of crimes by increasing the number of officers in high crime areas. In the past, there has been no satisfactory method of separating the impact of some major crime prevention from the effects of other factors. It has been hard to determine whether increased resources devoted to police presence would indeed reduce the crime rate. The procedure that will be introduced in this program is the collection of data on the percentage and rate of specific crimes, such as burglaries and car thefts, according to police presence in specific areas. As the department plans its evaluation process, it considers "the number of common crimes per neighborhood. Changes in this rate, over time, may indicate the impact of their officer increase in given areas.

The Program Logic Model

A logic model is a depiction of the flow of materials and processes for reaching the desired results of a particular program or organization. Think of it as your program or organization in a nutshell. It provides a bird's eye view of the entire program or organization by defining what resources will be put into a given project, how the project will be carried out, the expected short-term and long-term results, and how results will be measured. Logic models can be useful not only in grant proposals, but also for planning and analysis.

Typically, logic models are set up like a table and use the following terms: inputs, activities/processes, outputs, outcomes and evaluation. Terms vary, however, so don't worry about using and committing the "correct" terms. It's more important that you have a general sense of what the terms mean, and even more important that you are consistent in your use of them.

Logic Models, Piece By Piece

Increasingly, organizations across public, private, and voluntary sectors are being challenged to demonstrate the effectiveness and efficiency of their programs, and to be accountable to managers, funding agencies and taxpayers. One tool that can help organizations achieve these tasks is the program logic model, a diagram that provides a road map for a given program, showing what it is supposed to do, with whom, and why. The program logic model can help organizations to take their program evaluations a step further by involving stakeholders in considering not only whether objectives are achieved, but also whether programs address problems that are appropriate for the particular program and organization.

Programs are responses to situations. Homelessness is a situation. Services to transition people from homelessness constitute a **program**. The time, money, people, materials, and equipment needed to offer and manage the transition are the **inputs**. The inputs are converted into activities, services, or products, **outputs**, which reach the people whose needs are being addressed. These outputs are intended to result in changes or benefits for individuals, families, groups, communities, organizations, or systems. **Outcomes** may be measured as shorter term to longer-term achievements that result in human, economic, civic, or environmental impact.

Outcomes may be positive, negative or neutral; intended or unintended. These program elements are laid out in relation to the situation and the need that gave rise to the program. Outcomes are intended to result in a positive change in the originating status. However, situations are not static, so the originating situation that gave rise to the program is likely to change over the course of the program. It is, therefore, important that the outcomes of a program are subjected to scrutiny that will allow an nonprofit and its community of support to have a clear idea how a program "worked."

What is a Logic Model?

A logic model is:
- A picture of the program
- Simple representation of the program "theory" or "action" which explains the program and what it is to accomplish
- Shows relationship between what is put in (inputs), what is done (outputs), and what results (outcomes)
- Sequence of "if-then" relationships
- Core of program planning and evaluation

How a logic model is developed depends upon variables such as whether or not the program being planned is an existing one that needs definition, revision or a new focus. For an existing program, the logic model may begin with the existing inputs and outputs to be certain that there is a logical process occurring between these factors and the desired outcomes. In these cases it is good to ask such basic questions such as:

- "What is it that we do?"
- "What are we hoping to accomplish?"
- "What does our program consist of?"
- "Who are we reaching?"
- "What results are we seeking?"

If you are in the planning stage of a new program, you might start with the long-term expected end result--the impact - and work backwards.

- "What is our long-term desired result?"
- "What will be different as a result of this program?"
- "What must happen in each preceding step to get us there?"

A logic model is dynamic. It will change as the program changes. Much of the value of the logic model is found in the process of creating it, checking it, and modifying it. It is an iterative or incremental process that involves stakeholders working together to clarify underlying assumptions, expectations, and the conditions under which success is most likely.

Why use a program logic model?

The program logic model has many uses, including:

- facilitating program planning and delivery
- enhancing buy-in and team building among program stakeholders and participants by promoting participation and ownership
- aiding stakeholders in understanding the goals, expectations and outcomes associated with the program
- demonstrating how different components of a program, such as resources, activities and objectives, are linked helping to integrate program planning and evaluation through the identification of objectives and indicators
- focusing the evaluation through the identification of key issues and questions
- assisting in identifying unintended consequences of the program, and
- clarifying the causal assumptions and rationale upon which the program is based (for example, can the available resources be used to achieve the desired objectives?)

Common Steps toward Building a Logic Model

1. Form a small workgroup consisting of program planners, staff, evaluators, and other stakeholders. This group will likely need to meet several times to develop and revise the model.
2. Set boundaries for the program: for example, focus on a particular target group and recognize resource limitations.
3. Conduct a review of program reports, planning documents and relevant literature.
4. Make a list of project goals.
5. Define the target group(s): be as specific as possible (consider socio-demographic variables, health characteristics).
6. Outline the program's process or implementation objectives: what will the individuals who implement the program do?
7. Outline the process indicators: how will you know if the program activities have been implemented as planned?
8. Outline immediate and intermediate objectives: what are the desired short-term outcomes of the program? Objectives should include a direction (increase, decrease, alleviate, expand, etc.), and be specific, measurable, realistic, and based on rationale such as a review of the literature or previous experience.
9. Determine immediate and intermediate indicators or outputs: how will you know when your short-term objectives have been achieved?
10. Outline the long-term objectives of the program: what are the desired long-term outcomes of the program? Are they consistent with your organization's vision?
11. Determine long-term indicators or outputs: how will you know when the program's long-term objectives have been achieved?
12. List the project activities: what is the program intended to do in order to achieve its objectives? Activities should be driven by objectives rather than determining the objectives based on planned activities.
13. Group program activities into components or strategies (activities that fit together conceptually) such as counseling, social marketing, training, advocacy, coalition building, and educating.
14. Check your logic: is each element of the model causally linked to the next? Are causal linkages realistic? Are objectives clear and measurable? Are activities clear and measurable? Are there other potential activities for achieving the outcomes? Are resources adequate?
15. Verify your logic model with stakeholders and program staff who are not a part of the workgroup and modify accordingly.

Review the following logic model in order to identify the inputs, processes, outputs and outcomes in order to see how, logically, these factors relate to one another.

Program: Neighborhood Organizing

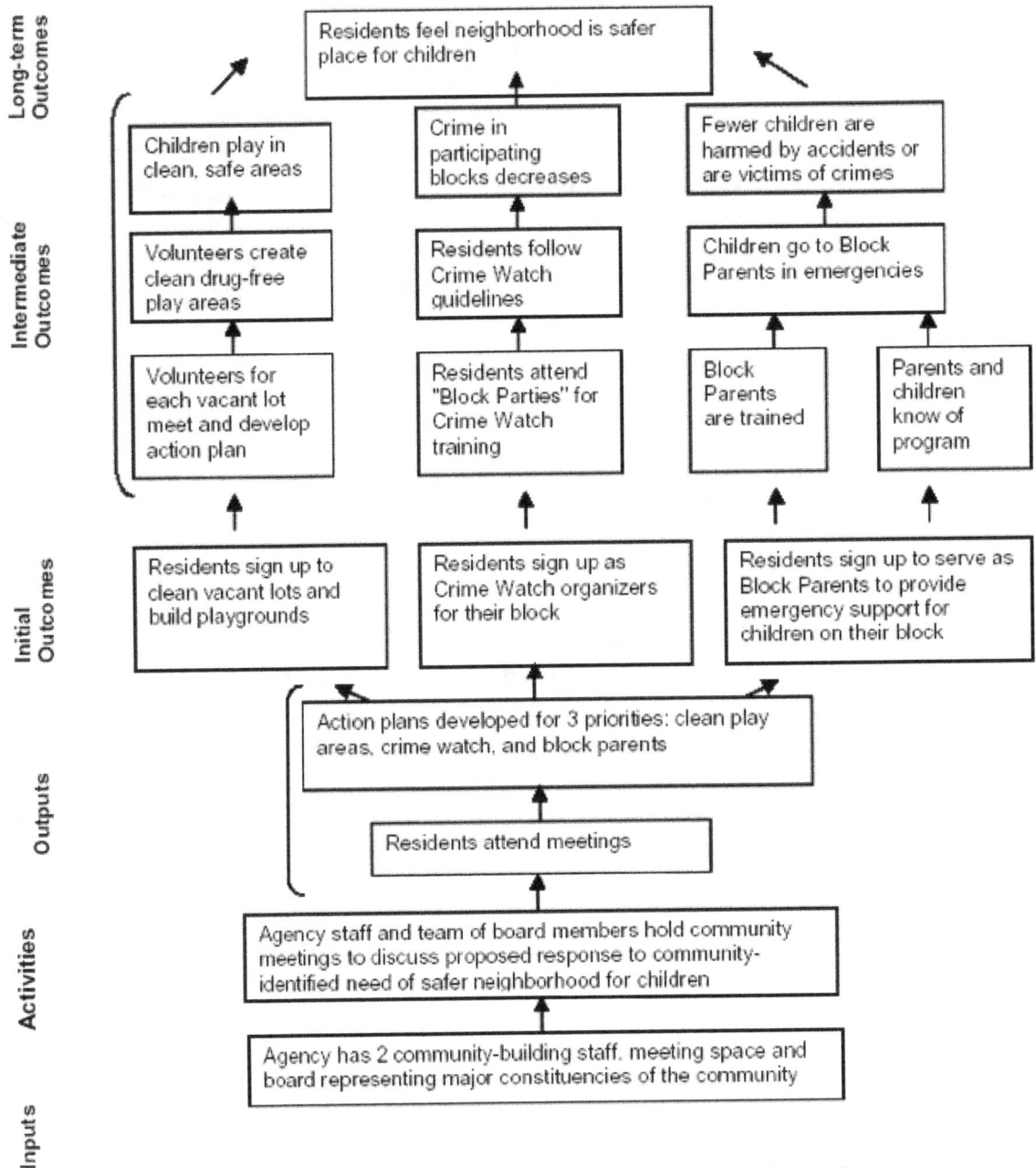

Long-term Outcomes

Residents feel neighborhood is safer place for children

Intermediate Outcomes

Children play in clean, safe areas	Crime in participating blocks decreases	Fewer children are harmed by accidents or are victims of crimes
Volunteers create clean drug-free play areas	Residents follow Crime Watch guidelines	Children go to Block Parents in emergencies
Volunteers for each vacant lot meet and develop action plan	Residents attend "Block Parties" for Crime Watch training	Block Parents are trained / Parents and children know of program

Initial Outcomes

Residents sign up to clean vacant lots and build playgrounds	Residents sign up as Crime Watch organizers for their block	Residents sign up to serve as Block Parents to provide emergency support for children on their block

Outputs

Action plans developed for 3 priorities: clean play areas, crime watch, and block parents

Residents attend meetings

Activities

Agency staff and team of board members hold community meetings to discuss proposed response to community-identified need of safer neighborhood for children

Inputs

Agency has 2 community-building staff, meeting space and board representing major constituencies of the community

United Way. Measuring Program Outcomes. A Practical Approach. United Way of America, 1996, page 48.

The diagram may look very different from one program to the next. For instance, a parenting education program may be modeled this way.

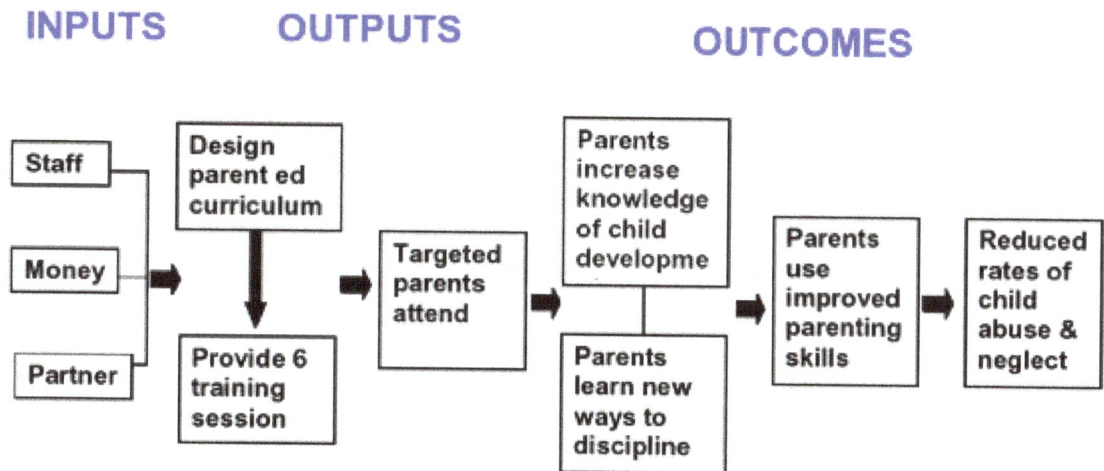

INPUTS　　**OUTPUTS**　　　　　　**OUTCOMES**

INPUTS	OUTPUTS	OUTCOMES
Staff	Design parent ed curriculum	Parents increase knowledge of child developme
Money	Targeted parents attend	Parents use improved parenting skills
Partner	Provide 6 training session	Parents learn new ways to discipline
		Reduced rates of child abuse & neglect

A logic model displays the chain of events that will effect changes and achieve your vision. You might think about this as a series of *if-then* relationships. For example:

If the program invests time and money, *then* a resource inventory can be developed. *If* there is a resource inventory, *then* families will know what resources and services are available. *If* they know, *then* they will be able to access the appropriate services to meet their needs. *If* they access the appropriate services, *then* their needs will be met. *If* partnering agencies contribute time and effort, *then* communications among agencies will improve. *If* communications among agencies improve, *then* there will be less overlap and duplication of services. *If* there is less service duplication, *then* freed-up resources can be used to address other needs.

Use the worksheet for the Logic Model in the Appendices to list inputs, outputs and outcomes as they are logically related to one another. Then use a blank page to draw a logic model of an existing or imagined program in which the processes are also diagrammed.

Inputs–

The materials and resources that an organization takes in and then processes in order to produce the desired results. Inputs can include people, money, equipment, facilities, supplies, and time—anything that is invested in the program.

Activities/Processes–

How your inputs will be put into action. Processes can be as simple as purchasing office supplies or as complex as manufacturing an aircraft. Keep in mind, however, that a logic model generally focuses on major processes that reoccur and work to produce a desired result.

Outputs–

The tangible results from major processes. They are often defined in numbers. For example, an output for a youth program might be to serve 100 new kids. Or an output for a community theater might be to purchase a new soundboard.

Outcomes–

The long-term impacts that your program will have on your organization as a whole or the people that your organization serves. Outcomes are often measured by an increase or decrease in a particular activity, such as capacity, revenue, skills, etc. Outcomes are the ultimate goals that you hope to reach.

Evaluations–

A brief description of how you will measure success. For instance, if your goal is to increase attendance at your after-school program, your evaluation might be the number of kids who attend on a given day.

Examples:

Logic models can be very simple or quite complex. Here are two examples:

Example 1:

OPERATION ANGEL TREE MINISTRY FLOW CHART

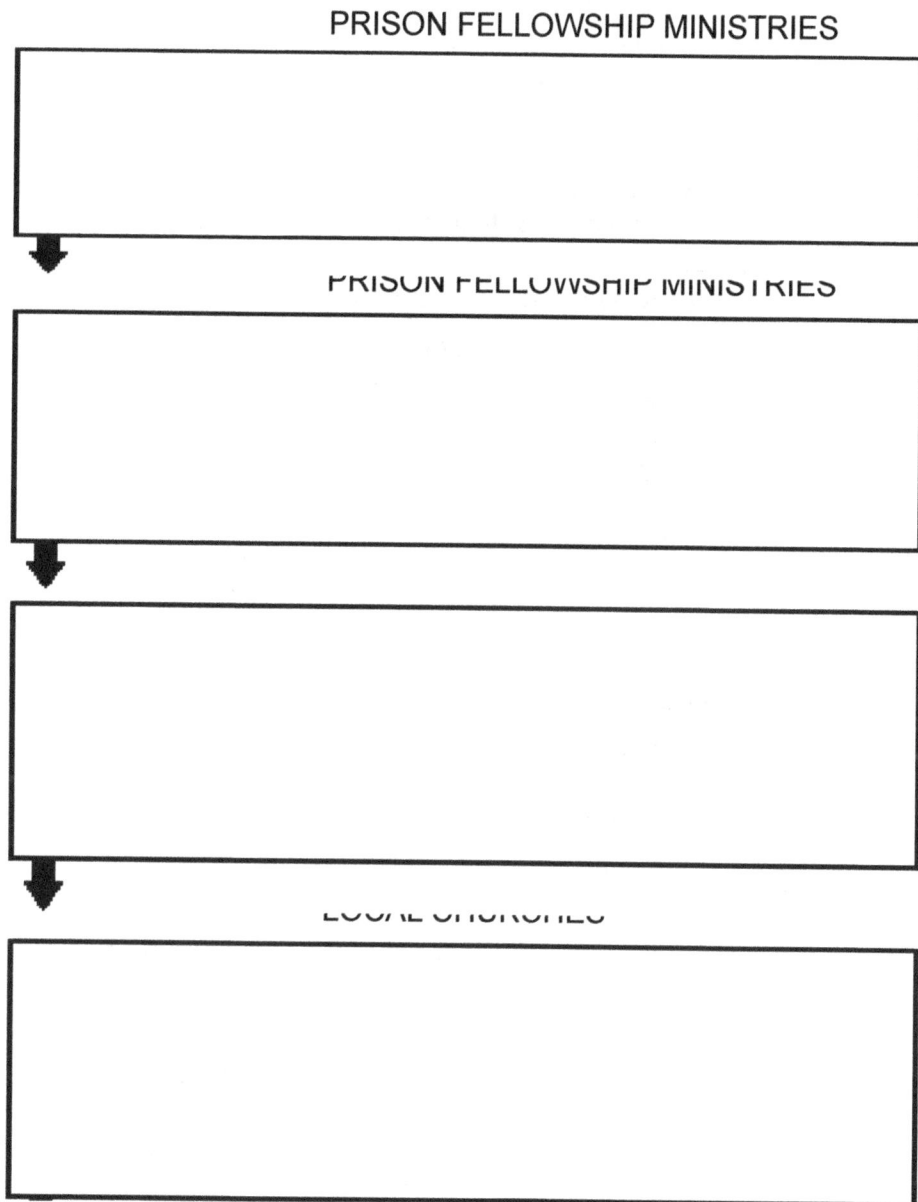

PRISON FELLOWSHIP MINISTRIES

PRISON FELLOWSHIP MINISTRIES

LOCAL CHURCHES

Example 2:

Objective 1:
Expanding outreach into the public school system and private schools

Activities/Inputs	Outputs	Outcomes	Evaluation
Board time	Four school partnerships	Increased collaboration	Number of partners
Outreach Coordinator Time	More students participating	Increased capacity	Increased incoming funds
Salary and mileage		Increased revenues	Number of students

Objective 2:
Enhancing our ability to raise funds through re-alignment of job duties

Activities/Inputs	Outputs	Outcomes	Evaluation
Board time	Community partnerships	Increased collaboration	Number of partners
Director Time	New donors	Increased revenues	Increased incoming funds
Salary and mileage	More Students	Increased sustainability	Number of students

Objective 3:
Developing a Website

Activities/Inputs	Outputs	Outcomes	Evaluation
Staff time	Functioning website	Increased efficiency	Staff time on phones
Consulant Time	More students participating	Increased capacity	Number of students
		Increased revenues	Increased incoming funds
		Increased sustainability	

Details, Details
Does your evaluation:

- Cover product, process, or both

- Tell who will perform the evaluation

- Tell how evaluators will be selected

- Define your criteria for evaluation

- Describe your methods for gathering data

- Explain any tests or questionnaires that you plan to use

- Describe how data will be analyzed

- Show how the evaluation will be used for program improvements

- Describe the evaluation reports that you plan to produce

VI. Future Funding

This is the last section of your proposal. If you have not thought beyond the particular grant in question, now is the time to start. Obviously one foundation cannot flip the bill for your entire program. In order to complete this section, you need to consider this grant's part in your overall planning. You can use one of three approaches to this proposal section:

1. Future funding for the program through grants. If the program will continue after the grant runs out, how will you fund it? For this approach, you must describe your plan for funding the remainder of the program.

2. Future funding for construction or renovation. If your project involves construction or renovation, you'll need a detail list of costs for maintaining the new or renovated facilities, along with where the funds will come from. This is also the time to discuss any program expansion that might result, along with the funding source(s) for that.

3. Other necessary funding. If you are requesting funding to purchase a piece of equipment, or for some other non-recurring cost, you must specify the funds necessary to support this and identify where these funds will come from.

Future Funding: Program Grants

If you are proposing a new program or project, the continuation of an existing project, or an expansion, your financial planning must go beyond the current proposed grant period. Few foundations want to adopt you over the long haul.

So where will you find funding in the future? This is an important question—for the funding source and the future of your organization. A new or expanded program becomes part of your organization. If the program works well, you would hate to see it come to an abrupt end due to lack of funds. Such an unfortunate event would affect your clients, your staff, and the reputation of your organization.

To improve your prospects, think of your program as a vital part of your organization's future. Consider as many ways possible for securing funds in the future. Do not gloss over this section with a statement such as, "We will continue to seek funding for this important community outreach." Prove the importance of the program by showing your reader that you have a plan.

"I'm living so far beyond my income that we may almost be said to be living apart."

– e. e. cummings

Here are some possibilities for funding your program after the grant period ends:

Option 1: – Becoming Self-Sufficient:
If your organization is large enough, and better yet successful, it might be able to assume future funding responsibilities. Showing evidence that you have done this with past programs is the best proof of your ability to do it again.

Option 2: – Changing a Fee—eventually:
If your program has the potential to eventually charge clients for services, such as a counseling center that works on a sliding scale, then describe your potential client population. Include information about income levels, research of fees for comparable services, and some evidence of client willingness to eventually pay. Use the data to project anticipated revenue over the course of the grant period. If your grant is to continue past one year, show how client fees will replace some of the second-year grant.

Option 3 – Subsidies:

Consider any third-party payers that you might contract with in order to subsidize the services to clients in the future. Such relationships have the potential for becoming a strong future funding source.

Option 4: – Growing successful fundraising efforts or planning new ones:

Make use of any non-grant fundraising programs that are growing. The increasing income from this might cover part, or even all, of the program eventually. Based on your history of fundraising, what projections can you make to demonstrate your ability to raise money in the future to cover program costs? What new efforts can you make? What haven't you tried?

Option 5: – Profitable Services or Activities:

You might have a profitable service or activity that is growing at a rate that might eventually cover costs of running your program. This means doing a thorough assessment of the costs and benefits of such activities. This could include contractual relationships, such as selling books and magazines at a profit and render your services at a loss. Perhaps you plan to expand your publications sales. If so, what degree of expansion can you afford? How much can you expect to gain by expanding the service? Is it enough to cover the program?

Option 6: – Applying for federal funding:

Applying for membership with an intermediary organization (like the United Way), in order to access federal funds can be quite beneficial. Have you checked into it? What are your chances for acceptance? Once accepted, an association may include your program in their yearly budget allocation.

Option 7: – Other organizations:

If your program is successful, it's possible that another organization could assume the financial or program responsibility. For example, if your program compliments services offered by your local school district, they might incorporate it into their budget for the future.

Remember, we advocate a broad diversity of funding sources!

You may be saying to yourself, "I can't guarantee that the school district will adopt my program or fees will eventually cover the cost." Proposal reviewers understand that a guarantee of future funding is unlikely. What they want is to know that you have considered the future of your new program and how it will stay funded. Remember: The more precise you are in your proposal, the more confidence that the funding source will have in you.

This statement would NOT evoke much confidence:

> In order to continue our program beyond 2009, Lets Go Shopping Clothing Service will make every effort to seek funds from other sources. Some options include revenue sharing funds, anti-recessionary funds, and any other funding source that we might qualify for.

The next statement is a bit more specific but still lacks the elements needed to inspire confidence:

> Built-in Babysitter Daycare was designed as a demonstration model. In the future the most successful component of the program will be packaged and made available to other sectors of the Poor County and other surrounding communities. Our intention is that this service will be continued and funded through Community Development Grants, Federal Urban Action Grants, HUD, Community Services Administration, local schools, and the United Way.

Below is a much better example. This statement shows well thought out commitment to future funding.

> The amount requested above will be used as "seed money" to begin the Luv 2 Read literacy project. If the program proves successful, it will clearly require additional funding.

> At this time, we are planning to seek funding support in the following ways:

> **1. Donations from groups and organizations currently involved in the project:**

> a) The Bookworm County School District has provided space for the program at each of their nine elementary schools. Over a dozen teachers, parents, and aides have also given of their time by volunteering as reading tutors. At a recent school board meeting it was decided that $10,000 would be allotted

to Luv 2 Read for the 2009-2010 school year if it is successful after the 2008-09 trial.

b) A local parents' group, Parents for Quality Education, has pledged to raise a minimum of $10,000 annually for Luv 2 Read. This group has had great success in the past with similar programs, including our teen peer-tutoring program. The attached letter reveals the community support that has already been shown for this new project.

2. Funding from the United Way: United Way has agreed to consider this project for continuous grant funding through Funds for Education, based on our first year's success.

3. Through relationships with other local organizations: The major bookstore chain, Books Express, has committed to the donations of books, incentive rewards (gift cards, free books, etc.) for the first year and will continue, based on the first year's results. At this time, they are considering a monetary donation after this grant period.

This plan shows guarantees of continual funding, commitments if the program proves successful, and possible funds. It reveals that the applicants have taken the time to make contacts and have already formed solid relationships within their community. The attached letter praising their programs adds to their potential as well.

Future Funding: Construction or Renovation Grants

When it comes to future funding for facilities expansion, whether for a new building or renovation, you need to consider three questions:
1. What will it cost to maintain this facility?
2. Are you planning any program expansions?
3. Where will the funds come from?

The Kresge Foundation is one of the largest foundations in the country that focuses on grants for construction and renovation. They specifically ask for the following:

> *Anticipated annual operating and maintenance costs of the project and source of the funds to meet such costs (If a special operating endowment is planned for the project, specify the total goal for endowment and amount presently raised towards that goal).*

When Kresge conducted a survey of their grantees, several of the questions raised, as well as the answers received, suggest that this foundations perspective and concerns are typical of sources that fund construction projects. Here are some examples:

> *Question: "Have there been any substantial revisions in project usage since completion? If so, outline reasons and results."*

Almost 87% of the respondents reported that no revisions had occurred. Of those reporting some variation in use, the most frequent reason given was a change in or expansion of the program's emphasis. Only one grantee indicated that the facility was no longer in use (in this case the institution no longer existed).

> *Question: "Have project operating and maintenance costs (exclusive of uncontrollable costs due to inflation, etc.) been about what you expected? In answering, please give the source of payment of operating and maintenance costs."*

Eighty-two percent answered yes. Approximately 8% said it was too early to respond to the question or made no comment at all. Of the approximately 10% who replied no, higher utility and heating costs were the most frequently mentioned problem. Even though the questionnaire specifically stated that uncontrollable costs due to inflation should be excluded as a factor, nearly 17% of all respondents mentioned inflation as their single most overriding problem in meeting operating and maintenance costs.

Construction of new facilities and expansion of existing building can do damage in a nonprofit organization. Careful planning is a must if you want to insure that the future costs of operation will continue with the help of secure sources. We do not recommend applying for this kind of grant unless you know that these costs will be covered. If program expansion is implied, planning must extend far into the future to avoid a vision of empty buildings and cancelled activities.

Covering Other Necessary Funding

Let's say that you are asking for funding to purchase equipment. You need to consider what else you might need in order to use that equipment. For example, if you are seeking funding for computers you will also need printers, ink cartridges, TONS of paper, antivirus software, etc. If your requested funds are for a new school bus, you will need to cover insurance, a driver, gasoline, maintenance, and other costs associated with a vehicle. If you need a special piece of machinery, will your staff need training in how to operate it? All details lead to questions on how additional costs will be paid for.

If you are requesting money for something non-recurring, such as research or planning, what provisions have you made for utilizing the new information obtained? In the case of planning, how will you obtain funds for implementation once the plans are made? For research, how will you compile your results? How much will it cost to publish your results? Who will receive and compile them? Chances are, every step in this process will cost money. Where will it come from?

Details, Details
Does your plan for future funding:

Show promise of future funding, should your program continue
Cover both maintenance and future program funding, in the case   of construction
Account for other needed expenses associated with equipment, vehicles, machinery, etc.

Completing the Proposal

Once the sections of the proposal are completed, other elements of the final presentation can be readied. These consist of a cover letter, a letter of inquiry (not always required) and the proposal summary (sometimes known as the Executive Summary or Abstract).

Letter of Inquiry

Sometimes called a Letter of Intent or Letter of Interest (LOI), this is not a part of the proposal. Rather, such a letter is a response to a demand by the funder that your initial approach should be a letter. The purpose of this letter is to provide a succinct picture of the program or project for which you seek funding

A good LOI cannot be composed before you have done all of the planning that precedes the actual writing of your proposal because until that planning is complete, your LOI will likely ramble. Without reference to the data accumulated during the planning process, the LOI will lack substance.

An LOI should contain a paragraph for each of the following and the aggregate should never exceed two pages.

1. Introduce your organization
2. Succinctly describe the project for which you are seeking support
3. A short statement to the effect that this new or expanded aspect of your work can't be funded through regular revenue streams
4. Statement of the total budget for the program or project and how much of that is being requested from the foundation or other funder you are writing to
5. Thank the reader for taking time to read your letter and provide your contact information

The LOI should be signed by the President of your Board or Executive Director of the organization. The signer's contact information should be provided in paragraph five. Should the funder agree to receive the proposal, further communication can be between the funder and the grant writer, but this initial communication needs to be from executive or board leadership. Finally, be certain that the LOI is sent on your organization's letterhead on high quality stock.

Your LOI should look something like this:

January 1, 2010

Mr. Charles Fox. Director
ABC Foundation
1 Main St.
Big City, NY 12345

Dear Mr. Fox:

I am writing to you needs. It was also noted that 59% of families seeking assistance do so for three or more years. While nutrition is not the only answer to poverty, research indicates that nutritional improvement may affect a student's ability to perform at school and may affect an adult's ability to seek, find, and maintain a job. Our current donor base is committed to continued funding for operational and food and acquisition and distribution costs and the community is generous in the contribution of food. No funds exist for the development of new services that may contribute to helping clients break the cycle of poverty. Our seeking of a grant from ABC Foundation is to meet the need for funds to begin this project.

Budget Total: $65,000. Proposals have been submitted to the US Department of Health and Human Services ($50,000), the DEF foundation ($20,000), and the Breakable Glass Co. Corporate Giving Program ($5,000). Each of these funding opportunities is highly competitive and is, therefore, uncertain as to the outcome of our proposal. At this time, we are requesting you to consider a full proposal of $40,000.

Thank you for your consideration. Poverty in Elm County will remain intractable unless innovative approaches are taken to address it. I will happy to provide further information as needed. Please feel free to call my office at (576) 234-5678 and to send a message to director@fpcec. org if I may be of service. Our vision, like your own, is grand and we are confident that we have placed our homes in the right hands.

Sincerely,

Sharon Wright
Executive Director

Cover Letters That Get Noticed

Your proposal should be accompanied by a cover letter, signed by the chairperson overseeing your project, or some other important contact person. This shows the foundation that your program is supported by your board. Even if someone else is in charge of the program that you are seeking funding for it is still a good idea to have the executive director (or the equivalent) sign the actual cover letter. Be sure to use your organization's letterhead.

on behalf of the Feed the Poor coalition of Elm County. Our organization was founded in 2005 in Elm City, NY for the purpose of improving services to those in need of primary and supplemental food provision throughout the county. Our vision is the eradication of hunger and poverty in our county. Members of the coalition include several church-based food pantries, community based food banks in the three cities with populations of over 100,000 each in Elm County, as well as the Department of Human Services. Overall, the population served totals 1,678,390, of which 35% live below 120% of the federal poverty level.

Our coalition has developed a project we call The Healthy Elm for the purpose of educating the clients we serve and the community as a whole in the principles of healthy consumption and the value of good nutrition. **Objectives: (1)** Provide nutritional counseling support at all food disbursement locations to encourage and support healthy eating habits, and (2) Include nutritional health information in all solicitations for food items.
Goals: (1) Train 40 volunteers to serve as nutritional support counselors by the end of 2010. (2) Increase the amount of donated food that has maximum nutritional value (whole grain dry goods, fresh vegetables for example) from the current 8% to 25% before the end of the year.
Outcomes: We plan to survey participants regarding school/work absenteeism rates, longevity of employment; income changes to above 120% of poverty level, and case load reductions in DHS.

Our annual evaluation process has revealed that although the coalition has successfully generated food donations in increasing amounts over the past five years and has coordinated the food's distribution processes in order to facilitate meeting increasing

The purpose of the cover letter is to briefly introduce and describe your proposal. This is in no way a substitute for the summary statement section of your proposal. The cover letter will not necessarily be read at the same time as the proposal so the summary is a crucial part of the proposal itself. Think of your cover as an introduction of who you are, what you need, and why it's important.

The cover letter is also the place to indicate your plan for follow-up. You could say something like, "We would appreciate the opportunity to speak further with you about our organization. . ." or "I will be in your area on (fill in the date) and would be happy to schedule a meeting with you."

A few things to avoid:

DON'T:

Show off your vast knowledge of the funding world - "Considering your deep concern for inner city teens we knew that our program would be of interest to you" might come across as condescending. That is not the way to catch the attention of a potential donor. Let the fact that you submitted a proposal for funding in one of their areas of their interest, speak for itself.

Tell your reader what to do - "We know that you will make this proposal a top priority," or "In light of our obvious need I'm sure you will (fill in the assumption)..." might trigger the exact opposite of what you want. Instead let them see the importance of your program for themselves.

Act desperate - Pitiful sign-offs like "Waiting expectantly," "Your humble servant," or "With a final plea" may come across as annoying.

Be impersonal - "To Whom It May Concern" or "ATTN: Potential Donor" are too generic for such an important correspondence. Be sure to address the correct contact person. When in doubt, ask. It would be embarrassing to address your letter to a woman who had been dead for twenty years (many foundations are formed in memory of someone) or is no longer with the foundation. Take time to double-check the spelling and any special details like Dr. or Sr.

Your cover letter should look something like this:

August 24, 2009
The Family Table Food Service
123 Services Ave.
Haven, IL 54321

ATTN: Charity Jones
The Save the World Foundation
1001 Giving Way, Suite 10K
Generosity, MA 12121

Dear Ms Jones,

I appreciate the opportunity to submit this request for funding in the amount of $12,000 for The Family Table Food Service outreach of Haven, Illinois. The Family Table goes beyond the typical soup kitchen or food pantry environment by serving home-cooked meals to the disadvantaged population of one of the Chicago area's forgotten communities. Haven, Illinois may sound like a cozy, Jeffersonian town. In reality, it houses the poorest of the poor. With an unemployment rate of 20%, and an average family income of $10,000 per year, most citizens are unable to afford the simplest of daily provisions. Rather than simply handing a family a bag of canned goods, we invite them inside for a family-style meal and lasting hope for the future.

Since our opening in November 2005, we have provided more than daily food. We have found a unique approach to our outreach. Local restaurants and grocery stores generously donate necessary food. During each meal, tables are hosted by local professional volunteers who can offer advice on everything from resume writing and interview etiquette to finding affordable housing and employment in some of the more promising surrounding towns. In the past 4 years, we have shared with over 100 individuals, couples, and families to get their lives moving in a new and exciting direction.

In today's troubling economy, we are seeing even more families reduced to below poverty level. The need for help and hope is greater than ever. For this reason, we are currently seeking funding in order to make it possible to expand our services even further. In addition to our on-going operational costs, we hope to enlarge our facility in order to add a childcare service for men and women in search of employment, and a small "store," known as the Community Closet, where the same individuals can find appropriate clothing for interviews and new jobs (clothing will be donated by Chicago businesses and offered at little or no cost).

Enclosed is a proposal, outlining our program and needs. If you have any questions or require further information, please don't hesitate to contact either my assistant Mary Albright or me at (212) 565-6556. Thank you in advance for your time and consideration. We look forward to hearing from you.

Sincerely,

Callmee Greatfull
Program Director

The writing of the grant is not the time to create and plan a program or project. It is a report regarding the planning and creating that has already been done.

The Introduction

The introduction is where you describe your organization's qualifications as a candidate for funding. When applying to a private foundation or a corporation, the introduction should be extensive. The reason for this is that your "credibility" may be the deciding factor when it comes to whether or not you receive funding. In a government proposal, you will seldom be asked for an "introduction." Instead, you may be asked for a "description" or "background of the applicant." This is their equivalent of an introduction.

"Information's pretty thin stuff unless mixed with experience."
–Clarence Day

What's does your name say about you?

For some people their name alone triggers an immediate response. Take Oprah for example. She doesn't even need a last name anymore. Her first name alone has a reputation for generosity, fun, power, and yes, wealth. Osama bin Laden on the other hand? Recognizable, even with the last name deleted—yes. Nice reputation—no.

The credibility of some organizations is carried, good or bad, by the name alone. If you hear the name "the Y'", you know exactly what they are about and what they provide. The same goes for MADD (Mothers Against Drunk Driving) and The American Red Cross. However, if you had a bad experience with any of these organizations the name might not trigger a touchy-feely reaction. One foundation reviewer might connect an organization's name with being financially secure, well managed, and providing needed services. Another might hear the same name and think "outdated" or "no longer providing what people need."

A first step towards developing credibility is examining whether you already have an "image" in society. You may need to work on reinforcing your already positive reputation. On the other hand, how will you defuse and negative press you might have received? Consider this while crafting your introduction.

What if your organization's name is not well known? Well, that could work in your favor or against you depending on what name you choose. If you have a home for runaways called "Lost and Found", you might wonder why some call you inquiring about lost bikes and kittens. A name like "Our House: Home for Teens" might be more appropriate—not to mention more appealing. You also don't want to sound pretentious, bias, or unintentionally comical (Take the Clean Up Your Act program for women trying to overcome addiction for example). You don't want to tarnish your image before you've had a chance to develop one.

Fashioning Your Letterhead

Nonprofit organizations often consider quality paper, professional letterheads, and brochures luxury items. Those funds could go toward someone's salary, or at least contribute to the new Air Hockey table in the youth game room.

While embossed stationery and spiral-bound four-color annual reports may fall into the "luxury" category, a presentation that is polished and easy on the eyes does not. It may even build your credibility to list the members of your board of directors (with their titles) in the letterhead if any are recognizable. Even without impressive names, you want the proposal to look top notch, even if you are a tiny organization that meets in someone's basement. Make it readable; include details like websites, e-mail, and mailing address; include your logo if you have one.

Items to Include in the Introduction

There is really no cut and dried formula for this section. The key is to outline your background, current activities, purpose, and goals for the future, who you serve, etc.

Your introduction might include:

- **The history of your organization**
- **Your purpose and values**
- **Goals**
- **Significant accomplishments**
- **Major activities**
- **Whom you serve**
- **Organizations that you are affiliated with**
- **Your funding sources**
- **Endorsements or positive comments about your programs**
- **The results of important evaluations**
- **Quotes from letters of support**
- **Invitations to contribute to Legislation**
- **Important organization publications**
- **Other items that will reinforce your credibility**

Proposal Summary
Or Executive Summary… or Abstract

This will actually be the last section of the proposal that you write, as it sums up the entire package. In a foundation proposal, the summary should be the first few paragraphs that the reader sees. Remember: The summary is part of the proposal, not the cover letter. In a government application, there is often a space on the cover sheet where you will be asked to provide a summary.

- Make your summary clear and concise. It should include:
- Name and location of your organization
- A sentence or two on what makes you credible
- The reason for the grant request (the problem or need being met)
- What you plan to achieve through this funding
- Steps you plan to take in order to accomplish your objectives
- The total cost of the project
- Amount you are requesting

If a foundation requests a list of funds already committed, mention them along with a note that a more detailed list is attached.

Why is the Summary Important?

You need to include a summary for several reasons:

1. Funding sources ask for them.

2. When the contact person is scanning proposals, the summary may be all he or she reads before deciding whether or not to consider a program (all the more reason why you want a summary that is clear, concise, and presents all the information they need).

3. It is an opportunity to spark interest, even in a person who doesn't have time to read your entire proposal.

4. It frames your proposal, putting what follows into context. The reader will get the point without having to read page after page. A good summary will make him/her want to read on.

5. It allows you to express your ideas briefly and with clarity - a skill that you will need for all sections of the proposal, as well as cover letters and other materials like brochures.

An example of a BAD summary:

Each year countless infants are born addicted to drugs and alcohol because their moms abused substances during pregnancy. We at Clean Up Your Act strive to give pregnant women struggling with addition a place to recover so they can give birth to healthy babies and have more promising futures themselves. To learn more about our program and current needs, read on.

What is wrong with this paragraph?

1. It is way too short.

2. 2.It is vague and poorly written

3. Important information is left out, including location of the organization, credibility statement, current need, objective, and the amount of funding requested.

4. The "suspense" won't be appreciated.

Now an example of a GOOD summary

For the past ten years, the Project BLESS has implemented Prison Fellowship's Angel Tree program in Northern Nevada. This program works with the children of incarcerated parents both to help facilitate a relationship with the incarcerated parent and offer other support for these children. The children of incarcerated parents are an often over-looked and under-served population with a very specific set of needs; they are at a much higher risk of suffering from depression and other emotional struggles, having delinquency problems, and ultimately ending up in prison themselves.

Through the multi-faceted Angel Tree program, we help mitigate these risk factors and encourage these children toward a positive and productive life. Our program contains three parts: the Christmas program, where we partner with local volunteers to purchase and deliver Christmas gifts for participating children on behalf of their incarcerated parent; our summer camp scholarship program, where we send the children to a local camp for a week at no charge to the families; and our mentoring program where children are partnered with an adult mentor for year-round support. In 2008, we delivered Christmas gifts to over 600 local children and provided summer camp scholarships to five Northern Nevada children. Through increased community awareness and improved contact with Angel Tree families, we expect to increase the number of Christmas participants to 700 and the number of summer camp attendees to 15 for 2009-10.

In September 2006, Project BLESS was awarded a $50,000 capacity-building grant from the U.S. Department of Health & Human Services. This funding is helping to build our organizational infrastructure, which will strengthen and improve our ability to continue to deliver needed services to our local community. In order to prepare for this year's expected growth we are seeking funding in the amount of $10,000 to match the federal funds received. Our primary need is for general operating expenses that will allow us to further strengthen our infrastructure so that we may continue to impact the lives of prisoners' children in Northern Nevada. Our secondary need is for Christmas presents for the children. We leave it up to your discretion which area you may choose to fund.

This summary clearly outlines everything a foundation needs to know.

Details, Details

Are the following true of your summary?

1. It's at the beginning of the proposal
2. Identifies who you are
3. Includes at least one sentence that shows:
   - Your credibility
   - Your current problem
   - Your objectives
   - Your program's methods
4. Includes total cost of the project
5. Names funds already obtained (if applicable)
6. Specifies requested amount
7. Is brief
8. Is clear and concise
9. Is interesting to read
10. Makes the recipient want to read on

General Techniques
in Grant Writing

Gather your Information

Try this technique:

Ask everyone on your staff and board of directors, as well as clients that you have an especially good relationship with, to write and send you:

- The most notable accomplishment on your organizations record (a special event, a unique outreach, etc.)
- One thing that makes your organization credible
- What funding will help you accomplish in the future

This will help you build a credibility statement.

Keep Current

If you don't already, begin keeping a list, (and have your staff do the same) to keep a file of all credibility-related information, such as:

- Organizations that request your services
- Individuals receiving or who have received help
- Successful projects

Not only will this help when writing your proposal, but your good record keeping will also add to your credibility.

The Importance of Variety

A stream of quotes and statistics will end in a dry, boring proposal. Simply listing achievements may cause your reader to lose interest as well. Think balance when writing your proposal. Come up with a creative, attractive way to present your figures and quotes. Weave some into the narrative while listing others in bullet points. Choose your most impressive quotes. This will allow you to present a great mix of client support and proof that you are making a difference in a way that is enjoyable to read.

Catch and Keep the Reviewer's Attention

The introduction is your chance to grab the reader's attention—or lose it before you ever get to the impressive parts.

With that in mind ...

DO
- Open with a sentence that makes them want to learn more (client quotes make great openings)
- Give a brief history of your organization
- Include some statistics and quotes
- Share recent accomplishments and evaluations

DON'T
- Bore your reader with the long drawn out "life story" of your organization
- Include a lengthy description of how your organization works
- List every grant you have applied for or received lately
- Use this as an opportunity to "preach" your organization's philosophies
- Sentimentalize

Keep in mind that your proposal might be the 20th that the reviewer reads that day.

Here are a few examples.

This introduction would be considered heavy on the philosophy and sentiment.

Introduction:

Buddy 2 Buddy is a nonprofit outreach that recognizes and addresses the needs of at-risk pre-teens. We believe that we make the greatest difference by providing these hurting children with a friend rather than a drill sergeant. With this in mind, each boy or girl is matched with a volunteer "buddy" who acts as both a mentor and supportive friend. The relation grows through one-on-one time activities, to the point where the child trusts his/her buddy in a way that would have been impossible in a strict, boot-camp-like environment. Problems are identified and relationship issues addressed. Most importantly in our opinion, these children who have experienced so many hard knocks discover a new sense of self-worth. Each child also receives necessary services, such as counseling, intervention, etc.

At Buddy 2 Buddy, no child is "a lost cause." They are simply children who are going through a tough time and need some guidance in order to grow into the responsible, productive adults they are all capable of becoming.

The above example does include important elements (identifying a very real problem and how they are meeting the need) but backs it up with opinions rather than facts.

Here is one example of one that is long on rhetoric. We spare you the entire introduction – it goes on for eight pages in its original form.

Introduction:

In spite of decades of educational reform and "improvements," little progress has been made in creating an educational environment in which students achieve noteworthy scholarly success. In a country so technically and economically advanced, our future generations are crushed under the weight of social burdens. They stand as monuments of our own inaction and methodical self-repair.

The entire proposal reads this way. While it makes a good point the word choice (not to mention the length) is much too heavy handed.

Now, for a good example:

Introduction:

Arts Today recently recognized Diablo Youth Symphony and Chorus as "The birthplace of tomorrow's virtuosos." In the past two years, 90% of our concerts have sold out. Season ticket sales have increased from 110 to 375 in the past year alone. These are promising numbers for a program that begin as a series of after school classes through a local community center.

Since our formal debut in 1992, DYSC has grown from a small performance group to a 200-voice chorus and full-scale orchestra. Our soloists, musicians, and smaller ensemble members have gone on to perform on Broadway, with the San Francisco Symphony, and at the White House. We have been honored to see our teens accepted at Julliard and other notable performing arts programs. In June 2009, DYSC has the privilege of performing at Symphony Hall as part of the America's Best Arts Festival.

Our commitment to excellence has gained us the endorsements of artists like Sarah Brightman, Richard Foster, and the Celtic Woman vocalists. As a result, our financial support has grown considerably, including a grant from . . .

Clearly, this is an amazing program with integrity and promise.

Here is another good example, using a different type of program.

Introduction:

To Your Health (accessed by calling 1-800-PROBLEM) is a call center for anyone seeking immediate answers to their medical questions and concerns. Since our founding in September 2007, over 100,000 seniors, teens, mothers, and other adults have been served in the privacy of their own homes. The goal of To Your Health is to enable patients to care for themselves whenever possible, and to increase knowledge of when to visit a doctor or other professional.

Initially funded by the American Medical Group, Our State Board of Doctors, and Medical Pros United, the program has grown from a local service in the Central Bay Area, to a statewide service. In addition to our 24/7 call center (manned by retired doctors and nurses and professional volunteers) we have teams available for talks, Q&A sessions, and medical fairs at schools, senior centers, and community events—all offered free of charge.

The average American lacks the ability to distinguish when a medical issue needs professional attention or can be solved with home treatment. As a result, serious problems like heart attacks go untreated while someone else called 911 for a minor nosebleed. Dr. Sylvia Smart of Medical Pros United, called our program, "The greatest service since Urgent Care clinics."

To Your Health operates as a 24-hour call service, offering advice and assistance on everything from infant first aid to mental health crises. Calls are toll free and completely confidential. A teen girl who has reason to believe that she might be pregnant, the mother concerned about how to keep her 5-year-old's lice from spreading to the entire family, or the senior citizen who is experiencing depression, questions can be answered in a private, safe environment. Unnecessary trips to the doctor are reduced. Other times potentially life-threatening conditions receive the attention they need.

On September 1, 2007, this program was made available to the residents of Footlong County and its surrounding cities—covering a population of 250,000. Six months later To Your Health had phone centers throughout the state of California. Today our phones not only ring around the clock but we have a constant demand for community talks and visits. At this time, we are in the process of developing a DVD series to make available in doctors' offices.

Although a bit wordy, this introduction is well written and interesting to read. The support of the medical community and the public response lend credibility to the program.

Time to Transition

As with any good writing, a well-crafted proposal moves logically from one thought, paragraph, or section to the next. In the introduction, you made the case for your program. Now it's time to move on to specific problems, needs and concerns that your proposal deals with.

In the previous introduction, the last sentence leads into a proposal for funds to produce a DVD series. This gives the reviewer an idea of what to expect next.

Annual Reports

Periodic reports on your organization, produced each year or every few years, are a valuable addition to your proposal introduction. While the proposal should be brief, a periodic report can go into greater detail if enclosed as an attachment with your proposal.

What if you Need Funding in More than One Area?

If you are seeking funding in more than one area then you will need to write individual proposals accordingly. Be sure to focus on your credibility in the area for which you are seeking support. If you are a non-profit mental health organization and seeking funds to train counselors and staff of a new and similar program, provide evidence of your capacity to train. If you wish to conduct research, give some reason for the reviewer to believe you are capable of conducting a research activity. If you are asking for support for a specific purpose other than operating support, keep related specifics in mind as you develop your introduction, and build a case for your ability to accomplish your objectives.

What If Another Organization Is Involved?

If some of the work you propose is to be conducted by an organization other than your own, you must provide evidence of that organization's credibility as well. Avoid linking up with anyone whose credibility falls short of your own. In some cases, the credibility of a reputable subcontractor may enhance your own credibility. When you involve another organization in your plan, make sure that you attach a letter from the organization guaranteeing its role in the program.

Letters of Support and Endorsement

Supporting letters can enhance your proposal and the value of your program. If you have endorsement or support letters, limit how many you send. Make sure that they truly support your proposed need. The best letters will reflect knowledge of your work, enthusiasm for your program, and an assurance to be of some kind of assistance should the proposal be funded.

Support letters should not be an obvious response to a solicitation for support.

"Gladys Howe of the Reformed Stalkers of Club County Support Initiative humbly requested a few words of endorsement, which I am pleased to provide."

They should be written to a specific director in your organization, and should include clear support of what you are doing. A letter filled with generalities might raise questions about how impressed they really are. If a letter contains a particularly noteworthy statement, include it somewhere in your proposal. Instead of saying, "Our program has received support from well-known community leaders (for details, see attachment)" include "Governor I. B. Incharge III said the following about our program" then insert a quote, followed by (full letter attached). Select support letters that will best support your need.

Details, Details

Does your introduction:
- Establish who you are
- Describe your purpose and goals
- Describe your programs
- Describe your typical clients
- Tell when you were established
- List accomplishments
- Include some statistics and quotes
- Support credibility in program area(s) you are seeking funding for
- Transition into problem or need statement
- Read easily
- Use clear language instead of jargon
- Make your point without rambling on

Conclusion

Now that we have bombarded you with information, remember these key points...

In order to write a strong proposal, be sure to:

- **Complete each required section**

- **Make each section as strong as possible, knowing that one weak link could make or break an opportunity for funding**

- **Refer to the proposal section checklists ("Details, Details") in this workbook to ensure that you have all the required elements**

Now you have the necessary tools for finding funding.

Good funding!

Appendix

If you have supporting documents to support your non-profit or program that do not fit into any of the previous sections, consider putting them into an appendix.

In previous sections of your proposal you can refer to the appendix (for example: for statistics see the Appendix A).

Here are a few examples:

Community Support

This appendix could include information that shows your ability to get your community involved. Incorporate things like:
* List of private sponsors – those who give out of the kindness of their hearts
* Support from local, regional, or national organizations (this would include media)
* Major corporations
* Other organizations that have or currently support you
* Letters of support from any of the above
*

Biographies
*
* Your board of directors along with brief bios on each member (good or bad, having one impresses people)
* Staff bios, especially directors and other key leaders in your program

What kind of information should you include in biographies?

* Photo
* Full name and title
* Occupation or job title
* Education
* Community involvement
* Brief life history as it relates to the organization
* Brief statement of beliefs and passions

[1] www.IndependentSector.org
[2] Code of Ethical Principles and Standards, http://www.afpnet.org/Ethics/EnforcementDetail.cfm?ItemNumber=3261
[3] For more on the Foundation Center visit www.fdncenter.org. They offer a variety of books and software.

These might also interest you:
- National Guide to Funding in Religion, 7th Edition May, 2003 ;1,690 pp. ;ISBN 1-931923-41-8; Price $155
- The Foundation Center's Guide to Grantseeking on the Web, 2003 Ed., September, 2003; 800 pp., Book: ISBN 1-931923-67-1; $29.95
- CD-ROM: ISBN 1-931923-73-6, $29.95 Book & CD-ROM, $49.95
- The Foundation Center's Database on CD-ROM, $1,195

[4] http://www.independentsector.org/programs/research/volunteer_time.html
[5] Rogers, Nino & Brenner Brown. Preventing Homelessness among People Leaving Prison, Issues in Brief: December 2003. Accessed online: http://www.vera.org/publication_pdf/209_407.pdf.

ISBN 978-0-9907441-8-4

51599

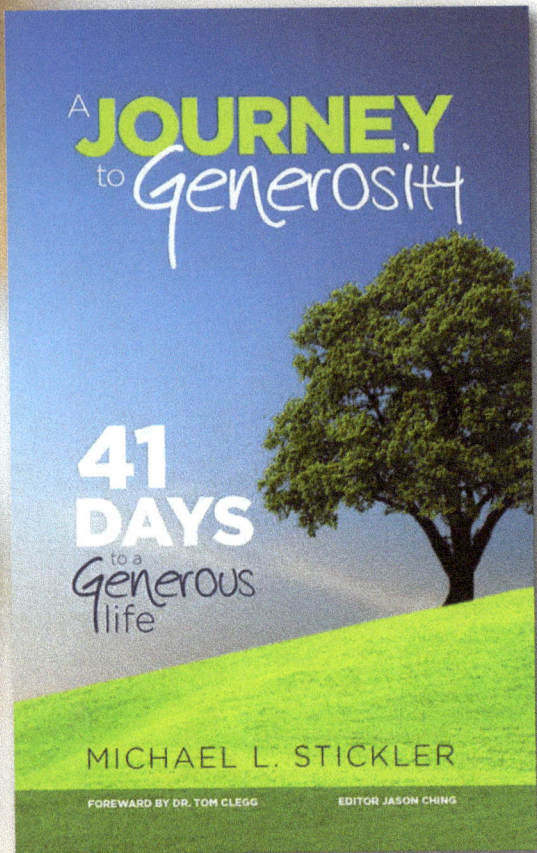

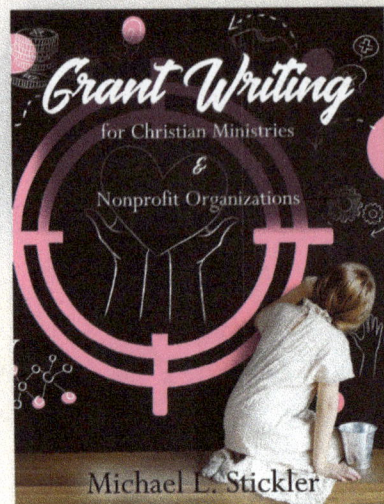

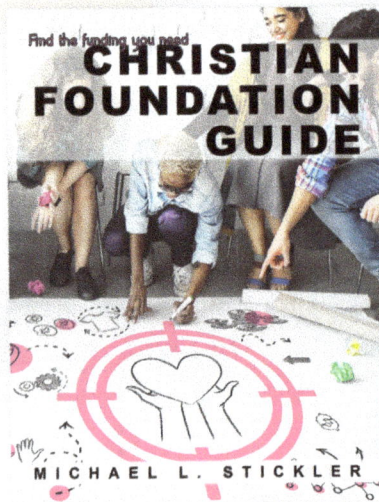

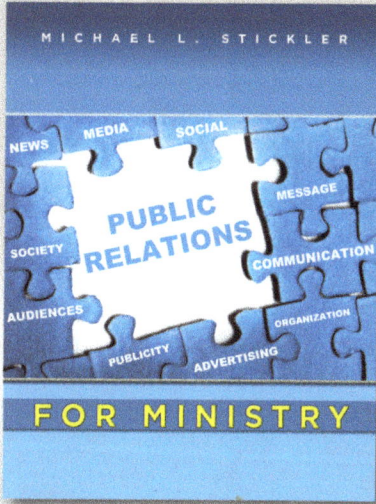

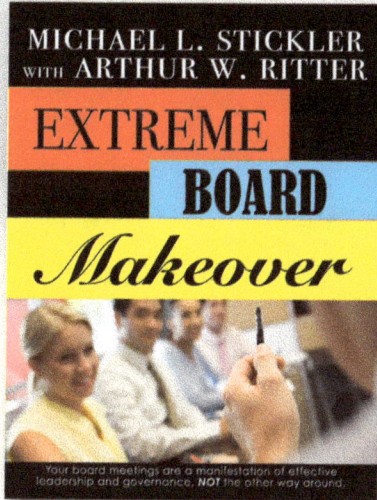

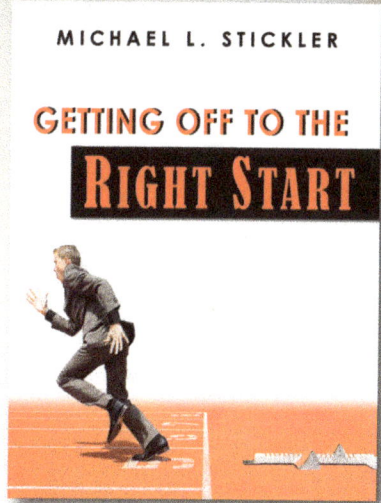

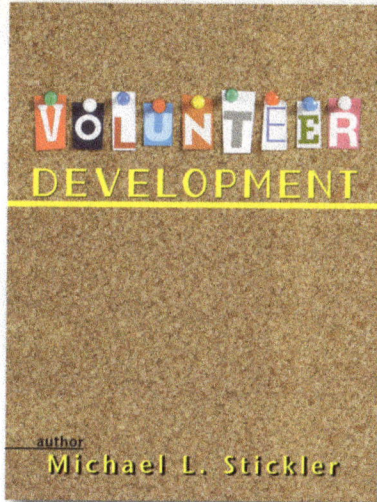

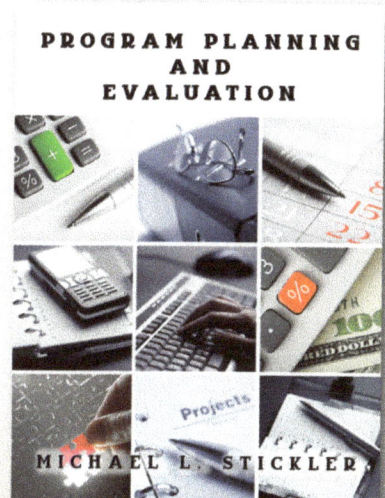

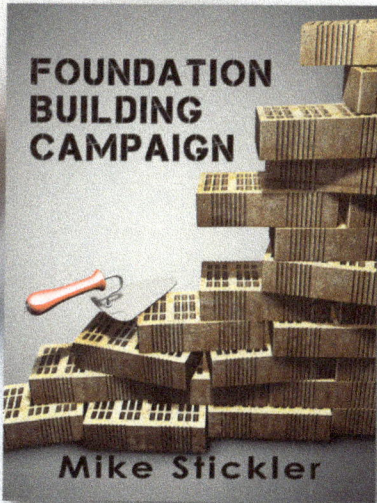

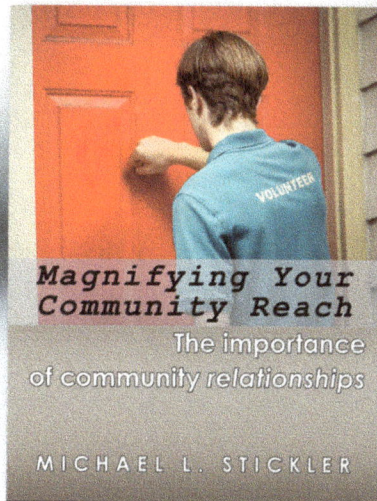

www.ingramcontent.com/pod-product-compliance
Lightning Source LLC
Chambersburg PA
CBHW080625030426
42336CB00018B/3085